BUSINESS PLANS TO GAME PLANS

A PRACTICAL SYSTEM FOR TURNING STRATEGIES INTO ACTION

JAN B. KING

EDITED BY JAMES WALSH

MERRITT PUBLISHING, A DIVISION OF THE MERRITT COMPANY

SANTA MONICA, CALIFORNIA

Business Plans to Game Plans

First edition, 1994
Second Printing 10/94
Copyright © 1994 by Merritt Publishing, a division of The Merritt Company

Merritt Publishing
1661 Ninth Street
Santa Monica, California 90406

For a list of other publications or for more information, please call (800) 638-7597. In Alaska and Hawaii, please call (310) 450-7234.

Library of Congress Catalogue Card Number: Issuance Pending

King, Jan B.
Business Plans to Game Plans — Taking Control
A practical system for turning strategies into action.
Includes index.
Pages: 350

ISBN 1-56343-071-1
Printed in the United States of America.

Acknowledgements

I am deeply indebted to many individuals and organizations who have provided an invaluable combination of professional expertise and personal support.

Much personal appreciation goes to the late Bo Merritt who founded our company, and all of the employees from whom I learn more about running a company every day.

Many of the concepts for and the development of the worksheets and their instructions came from one very talented consultant and partner with the Santa Monica, California, firm of Hankin & Co., John R. Loevenguth. John's years of experience with turnarounds and growing companies in transition provided wellness training for our very well company.

Particular recognition must also go to Dr. Ann Graham Ehringer and the members of TEC 81. TEC (The Executive Committee, based in San Diego, California) is an organization devoted to supporting CEOs.

Other collegues who gave me ideas, support, and critique are Bill Hawfield, Corey Schlossmann, John Nelson, and Bob Sullivan.

Business Plans to Game Plans is the third title in Merritt Publishing's "Taking Control" series, which seeks to help employers and business owners grapple with and overcome the host of extraordinary risks facing the modern business enterprise.

Upcoming titles will cover corporate finance, workplace diversity and business risk management, among other subjects. To keep these projects — and the series as a whole — well focused, the editors at Merritt Publishing welcome feedback from readers.

Business Plans To Game Plans Table Of Contents

Introduction: Our Game Plan

Many business books talk about business plans and strategic planning. Few tell you how to implement these plans. Why? Because the writers of business books focus on accomplishment, usually their own. They dream and forget about the hard part — the work it takes to gain success.

This book focuses on the hard part, because that's what leads to success.

And make no mistake, implementing a business plan takes hard work. It takes wisdom, discipline, courage, an eye for detail and — most of all — persistence. It also requires an outward focus. You must set goals, communicate them, review them, monitor their realization and stick to them when other people might abandon them.

Into the Breach

I know how hard these things are, and I know that they lead to success. In 1990, I found myself running a publishing company where I'd worked for seven years. In a matter of weeks, I had to grapple with a wide range of management problems; with little relevant experience and no formal business education, I had to learn to take control.

My company had been in business since 1957. I came to it as a writer and editor, then as the company's editorial director — a solid middle management position. Still, on the day I became president, I had never seen one of its financial statements.

In the months that followed, I talked to anyone who would listen. I overwhelmed some unsuspecting ears, but many more people helped me, giving me their experience and wisdom. Over time, they taught me to see the company as a series of four disciplines — *finance, marketing, product development,* and *operations* — and to develop a system for

The four basic disciplines

1

Simplicity of ends and means

setting up measurements and then monitoring how we performed in each area.

With regard to *finance*, I learned that the essential process involves setting projections that, in turn, allow you to monitor and manage cash, cash flow and profits — the things that keep you in business.

With regard to *marketing* — to many business people, the great unknown — it comes down to this question: Who wants to buy your product and how do you find these people?

Some managers consider *product development* part of marketing or operations. They shouldn't. How you create new products and refine existing ones says a lot about how you run your company and where it goes. Indeed, the manner in which you develop and improve your products communicates your corporate culture and vision more than anything else.

Operations entails more than just maintaining plant and facilities. It involves broad topics centering on these questions: How easy is it for your customers to get in touch with your company? How quickly do you get your product to them? How easy do you make it for your customers to pay you?

Socrates' Fool

It took me four years to learn these things. When I began, I was like Socrates' fool: I didn't know how much I didn't know. And like Socrates himself, as time went on, I discovered that it wasn't complexity that made for success. It was simplicity — simplicity of ends and means, as it were. We worked out kinks in marketing, production, and fulfillment, for example. We refined our corporate vision and mission statements to simplify them. I simplified the reports and key indicators I describe in this book, focusing them on things of importance and ridding them of everything else. Like so many other things we do, these had started out maddeningly complex, filled with all sorts of numbers and concepts. The longer I used them, the more basic they became.

More than anything else, I learned that in business, simplicity is the primary virtue; trouble and troublemakers hide in complexity. Simplicity became the benchmark for everything I did, the standard by which I judged the usefulness of what we all did. I faced a myriad of questions and problems every day, and I wanted them reduced to understandable form. I needed to make decisions quickly and effectively and get on to the next issue. I needed clarity. When I came to the office each morning, I had to understand how the business was doing on a constantly-updated basis. Equally important, I had to make sure the other employees knew how the business was doing so that they would work toward the objectives we developed.

Financial Tools

This brought me to an important question: How, exactly, could I let the employees know how the company was doing?

Because my company was (and still is) employee owned, the answer was to share financial information with all employees. I've heard the arguments against this kind of openness — the most compelling being that competitors can use this information against you. But I took employee ownership seriously and expected everyone at the company to help run our business. I couldn't expect others to do what I couldn't do myself — namely, run a business without knowing those numbers by which we measure success or failure. But I shared financials with my employees not for the sake of openness. I did it in the hope that they would see how the numbers sprang from their own work. I wanted my employees to grasp the numbers as proof of the importance to the company of everything they did.

In short, I gave my employees access to the financials and other documents so as to help them make intelligent decisions about their work. I educated them about what the numbers meant in the expectation that they would use those numbers not just to gauge our success but to guide their own action.

And I disovered the remarkable power you harness by doing this. Of all the memories I have of the early years, the one I value most came after I started circulating the financials. At a rather ordinary operations

Cause and effect

meeting, an employee suggested that we reduce inventory, saying that this would increase our cash position going into the critical months of our year.

It was an extraordinary moment. Consultants talk for billable hour after billable hour about inventory accountancy. On his own, this guy figured out that a tight inventory made the best use of capital for us. He didn't earn much; indeed, fully two thirds of my people earned more. But his income didn't limit his ability to comprehend the connection between inventory and cash. And his comprehension meant that my openness with the numbers had paid off.

It did not fail to register with me that when I had been an employee — better paid and supposedly better informed — I had not stopped to think about the impact of inventory on cash in the bank.

It also registered that, in sharing financials, I had changed my company fundamentally. Like many entrepreneurs, the founder of my company hadn't believed in sharing financials with his employees. We received monthly sales reports, of course. And the bonus program for managers depended on profits. I knew that profits depended on sales, and sales interested me insofar as it pleased me to see that the books I helped write actually sold. But sales seemed magical to me; I had no way to predict them. More important, I didn't think I could affect them in any immediate way. So I eagerly awaited the accountant's proclamation at the end of each year — to find out whether I'd get a bonus. I had no clue how I personally could affect sales.

The Direct Connection

It's hard for me to imagine this now, but as important as my work was to me, back then I felt no direct connection to the financial well-being of the company. As a writer, I took pride in the quality of my work. I believed that my skills added value to the company. I felt that my coworkers liked me and respected me. But I let other people — more inclined for that kind of work — take care of the business end of things. My bonus aside, it didn't occur to me to ask about the financials, and anyway, my job description said nothing about making money. Nor would I

4

have been interested enough to ask what our financials meant had I seen them.

In short, since I didn't understand the financial end of the business, I couldn't see how my job connected to the work done in the accounting department. I considered my coworkers there dependable people, but I didn't try to understand what they did behind their computers all day. What was important to me was that I could depend on them to get my paycheck out on time. Occasionally, at staff meetings, the CFO would ask us to hold down our spending. But this had little effect on my behavior, since my people spent money only on the occasional visit to clients or to attend seminars.

As for the marketing department, we always grumbled that it spent too much money. And as long as operations got our books printed and shipped on time, I was happy.

A Useful Naivete

In all, like many employees, I had no appreciation of what it takes to run a company. When I became president, this naivete served me well. I had no idea of the demands involved in running a company, so I never doubted I could do it.

Now I know that I should have been scared to death.

But I believed in the ability of people to do just about anything. I believed in business as a force for good in the world, and in the capacity — indeed, the desire — of ordinary people to find meaning in the activity of business and so contribute to society.

And when I became president of my company, I discovered that, like me, those who worked with me believed that we could turn a sleepy little company into a lean performer, poised for growth. We did that, with the help of the ideas put forth in this book. And now, because we enjoyed the hard work as much as the accomplishment, I want to share the essentials of how we went about it.

There have been many iterations of the formulas and worksheets in this book. And I'm sure there will be many more as time goes on. But they do make the

The central argument

5

central argument of this book — that a good business plan deserves to be implemented well, and that any reasonably bright person with enough commitment and concentration can make it happen.

How to use this book

I wrote this book to help other owners and managers learn what I did — but in a much shorter time. The structure of the book intends to help you consider tactics and set direction and budgets in the first three chapters and covers finance, marketing, product development and operations implementation in the last four.

Each chapter (beginning with Chapter 2) starts with a discussion of relevant concepts and issues. That discussion is followed by a series of progressive worksheets and explanations.

Each explanation consists of an overview, directions for the worksheet and suggestions for questions that will help you use the worksheet to its fullest extent.

These worksheets are intended to be used. Please copy them freely. Distribute them to as many employees as you think useful. You may want to copy them onto spreadsheet computer software. Whatever medium you use, the object of these worksheets remains the same — to help you take control your business.

CHAPTER 1:
TACTICS

Every coach knows that you don't win games in the locker room, drawing up beautiful plays. You win games on the field, where people execute your plays — sometimes not so beautifully.

But on the field, beauty doesn't matter so much as the score. You win if you know what it takes to win and then execute. In a game, this means outscoring your opponent. In business, it means many things — making money, dominating markets, providing products and services of value, making a contribution to society, giving others the opportunity to achieve success and security.

Whatever your goal, you set it out in a business plan, and because you care about that goal your business plan looks beautiful when you put it together. Then you start your business, and the real world intrudes. You discover that things don't play out as you imagined. You discover, in other words, the subject of this book: the difference between the business plan and the game plan — the difference between ends and means. You discover the necessity of adjusting the means by which you keep your operation headed toward its goals.

The Value of Information

To do this, you need good information — also the subject of this book.

Does a coach call the next play without knowing where the ball is on the field? No more than you can make a good marketing decision without knowing how your product sells now.

In the same way, you must know where and how the actual experience of your company deviates from the projections in your business plan — financially, in your marketing and sales efforts, operationally, and in your product development efforts. You must

The real world intrudes

The benefits of planning

know where you are in order to get where you want to be — before time runs out in the game.

To do this, you need both a business plan and a game plan.

According to a survey commissioned by AT&T in 1993, fewer than 42 percent of small businesses started operations with formal business plans.[1] Among businesses with revenues under $500,000, only one in three began with a formal plan.

Among small companies with written business plans, 40 percent found their projections so optimistic as to be useless once they commenced operations. Most of the others discovered their plans so incomplete as to be ineffective. Only two of three used balance sheets or profit analyses in their plans. Fewer still listed the products and services they offered, or pricing information. Benchmarks like cash flow, advertising and promotional spending and capital expenses showed up rarely, if at all.

Two in three small companies found their plans lacking because the plans didn't consider the factors most important to running a growth company — finance, marketing, product development, and operations.

Many small business owners in the survey attributed their success to investments in technology, employee training or marketing, not to any business plan. But among small businesses which experienced growth over two years, 59 percent based operations on a formal plan. Of these, 70 percent attributed their success primarily to this connection.

A Greater Prosperity

Clearly, few small businesses focus on long-term planning and — more important — implementing their plans. If they did, they would likely enjoy a greater prosperity. As the AT&T survey concluded:

---

[1]Few small business owners (fewer than one in ten, according to one survey) consider long-term planning important enough actually to do it. This shouldn't be. If the head person doesn't think about the long-term prospects, no one will.

A specific example of the benefit of planning by small business is the increased accuracy of financial projections. Accurately predicting income allows small business to create realistic and achievable programs for growth and expansion.

As the owner or manager of a company, you probably work alone to set strategy. You know your company and its business better than anyone else. You think about them a lot. You have a vision for your company, and you know this vision because you live it. But when you step out of your office, you meet people who may not share your vision. These people may fail to execute. Your vision may falter.

Without a plan, *you* may falter, because it's hard to make good decisions without a good framework.

And you need more than a business plan. You need a game plan. Business plans, as a rule, don't address critical issues like communicating your goals to employees and customers. They formulate broad goals, but they don't tell you how to set your business up and run it day to day so as to reach your goals. They don't tell you how to implement your business plan and measure your performance. They serve the needs of a different audience — bankers and investors. They don't help the day to day players executing your game plan — coworkers, customers and vendors.

If your business plan isn't on target, you won't get financing. That's an unfortunate loss of opportunity. But if your game plan doesn't work, your company might fail after it's started. You 'll end up losing a lot of money — your own and that of your investors.

The Guiding Principles

Several overriding principles will emerge from this book. Because they powerfully influence the way managers think about running their companies, these principles are worth considering at the beginning.

Your vision for your company

The critical details

1) Variance may mean trouble, so keep an eye on it.

Your business may outperform your projections. It may fall short. Either way, you need to know. A game plan allows you to monitor performance in detail, and so learn how performance varies from the vision of your business plan. There are no shortcuts in preparing the information, in studying it, and in acting on it. You must plan, act, measure, and plan again. Don't expect to do this quickly. Analyzing the data takes time — four times as long as it takes to compile the data, according to one rule of thumb.

2) Find the important details, and focus on them.

You must know all the details of your business — and you must know which are critical. You must study your operations, and then extract those details that are key to your success. It's not enough to house volumes of reports on a bookshelf. You must know what those reports mean. If, for example, you send out 50,000 pieces of direct mail and two weeks later sales jump, you may conclude that you dropped an effective mailing. But maybe your advertising kicked in at the same time, or perhaps a distributor launched an incentive program. You must find out so as to know what works and what doesn't.

And remember that data is about quantity, not quality. It measures performance by answering objective questions: How well do our results match up against our expectations? What's different? Is the trend up or down? Will these trends last a short time, or do they look long term? What might have contributed to what we see in the data? What's missing from this data that would lead us to ask more questions?

Data doesn't answer questions of quality: Is what we see good or bad? How important is what we see? How should we respond?

As a rule, the finance department is the one corporate unit devoted to quantitative analysis. It doesn't develop, produce, market or deliver the product. It measures the results of your efforts to do all that.[2] It provides you with the data from which you draw the benchmarks for measuring your company's performance. This doesn't make the financial department more important than the others — simply more useful in this context.

3) *Let reality inform your management.*

The problems you encounter in running your company are tough enough to solve. Don't let confusion muddy the waters.

This means keeping your analyses as objective as possible. Admit what you see to those around you. Don't try to persuade yourself or others to see what isn't there.

You may be the only person, for example, who can tell whether a two-month downturn in revenues reflects your ordinary business cycle or the beginning of a more drastic trend. Either way, you must gauge the truth and act accordingly.

4) *Set standards and give your employees the tools with which to meet your goals.*

Most employees feel responsible for meeting the objectives of their companies, and they like their goals simple and measurable. They also meet their goals when they have the tools to do so.

As their leader, you decide what's important and communicate this to your employees. Make sure your employees know your thinking; talk about what's important — a lot. Set goals and give your employees the tools they need to meet them.

You must also give your employees clear ways to measure how well they meet your standards. You define the standards by which your employees measure their work, and you enforce discipline when things go wrong. Some employers go about this by intimidating their employees. Others "empower" their employees — too often by giving their employees tasks to accomplish but no tools with which

---

[2]Your operations and product development departments answer qualitative questions.

The best report card

to do so. Employees respond positively when they know what their managers want and how they can contribute. They succeed when their managers enable them to do so.

5) *Lead by example.*

You send messages to your employees every day. You tell them what's important to you by the attention you pay to this or that detail, by the questions you ask and by the reports you request.

By stressing the ratios and measures you value — indeed, by showing a keen interest in these numbers — you focus your staff on the important things.

6) *Don't rely on experts. Take control.*

Complacent managers assume too many virtues in experts. They assume, for example, that an outside accountant will understand all the numbers that pertain to the business and alert management when the numbers spell trouble.

Active managers don't assume anything. They take control by making sure that they understand the numbers themselves. They know that numbers unlock the key to what happens daily at the office. They learn the stories numbers tell — of trends, of cycles. They understand that numbers even reveal what, as managers, they themselves do well and what they do poorly. They see numbers as their report card.

7) *Look to the long term — the very long term.*

You won't be around forever, so plan ahead.

This is sometimes hard to appreciate, especially if you founded your own company. But it's important. Making sure that your company survives you helps you and your employees focus on matters of importance.

Many companies run and even thrive on personality alone — on the charismatic leader whose employees rally round for direction and inspiration. Businesses like this can start to look more like cults than companies, though, and cult-companies often don't outlive their leaders. Companies thrive when they operate according to principles their employees can believe in. Your employees will do better if they believe that your company exists to do something more than make you wealthy. They want to know that their efforts will pay off whether you're around or not.

This does not take away from you, the person running the company, so much as it gives to your employees. You improve your own prospects for a payoff from your employees if you improve *their* prospects for a payoff from your company. If you show them that you expect your company to run whether you're there or not, you show that you really do look to the long term. If they do better, you do better.

The Bottom Line

In this book I want to show you how to turn a good business plan into an effective game plan. I want to persuade you of the importance of planning, acting, measuring, adjusting, and planning again — and provide you with ways to do these things. I ask lots of questions, some tough, and call for straightforward and useful answers.

I believe that most business books are like cheerleaders — they offer support but not much direct help when it comes to winning the game of business. You can draw energy from dreaming about the $50 million or $100 million or $1 billion company yours will become some day, but you can distract yourself, too. Whether you get that far depends on how well you plan and execute. In business as in sports, planning and executing are everything.

Above all, I want this book to be useful. I present tools to allow you to look inside the important areas of your company and assess where you are and what you must do to move forward.[3] Some worksheets are diagnostic tests for existing operations;

---

[3]This book doesn't cover two other management tools vital to long-term success — a compensation system that rewards on-target performance and the communication skills that create a work environment conducive to real employee participation.

Give employees tools

some give you an outline for future action. Taken together, they provide a disciplined system that keeps you moving ahead without reinventing the wheel.

I also want to argue the importance of every employee in this effort. I believe so strongly in the potential of every individual who works for my company that one of my goals as leader is to teach everyone how to run a company. I look at each employee as a potential successor, and seek to mentor that person as I would a son or daughter who might one day run the business. I don't hold back information; more important, I seek to share whatever wisdom I have gained.

I try to give my employees the tools with which they can make success their own—just as, in this book, I want to give readers the tools with which they can fashion their own success. These tools will help you do four things:

1) Develop vision and mission statements and set goals for your company;

2) Establish tracking systems in the critical areas of finance, marketing, product development, and operations to help you measure your success;

3) Learn by looking at what other businesses with similar challenges do; and

4) Become your own consultant by asking the right questions to look hard at what the numbers tell you, and to help you find creative solutions to your challenges.

Growth companies tend to be confident of their technical superiority to competitors but worry that their competitors have an edge in planning. This holds especially for small companies even though their competitors tend to be other small businesses.

Underlying this perception lies the fear that the small company operates at a disadvantage when it comes to planning and operational discipline. It also reflects the tendency to worry that any competitor comes to the game better qualified. Neither premise is true. Small companies can plan and execute as well as big companies; some experts think they do even better.

You can do the same with the right numbers and a willingness to concentrate on them. If you use the worksheets and forms in this book, you will have enough critical data to run your business successfully.

Critical data

CHAPTER 2: SETTING DIRECTION

Anyone who has ever started a business knows that by the second week of operation, issues unforeseen in the original plan begin to surface. Business begins and ends in the practical medium of the real world — the marketplace. And the marketplace defies easy prediction.

Business plans, by financial necessity, must set a broad target for the success of a company without knowing what day to day work will be like or what practical challenges will emerge. You need to find tools that apply management theory and your business plan targets to the practical challenges of running a company.

Game plans grow out of the business plans, but they need some coaxing. You get from one to the other by gradually bridging the gap and bringing into focus those things you must do to reach your goal. This chapter will take you through the focusing process. Its worksheets and exercises cover items which, by discovering the specific things your company must to do to succeed, turn the abstract into the concrete.

Getting From One to the Other

Note the progression. You set strategy in your business plan and tactics in your game plan. You get from one to the other — that is, from the theoretical to the practical — by monitoring and managing. The worksheets in this chapter help you do that. You use them not only to figure out what you must do to turn your vision into reality, but to measure your progress.

These worksheets let every member of your organization know what to do and when, and how everything fits together. This is key. Your game plan gives your employees a sense of purpose because it communicates to them what you have in mind — on the

Your game plan covers tactics

Focus on where you are today

very good theory that, if what you have in mind excites you, it will excite other people, too.

By identifying where you see yourself tomorrow, you create a well-focused picture of where you are today.

Giving Meaning to Work

When Sherry Sheng came from the Seattle Aquarium to take over as executive director of the Portland (Oregon) Zoo, she found a public entity that had lost a practical sense of the market it served. To revitalize the staff, she led all 100 employees through a rigorous self-evaluation aimed at giving meaning to their work.

Sheng used techniques more often found in the private sector than the public, looking beyond day-to-day operational concerns and creating a vision on which future decisions could be based. "You can call it strategic planning," Sheng told a local newspaper. "But it wasn't just to create some document. We needed to be able to draw out the passion of a place like this. People come to look at the animals because they get to you at a gut level."

She felt the same visceral passion could motivate employees. To capture this, she developed a vision statement for the Zoo. She worked with a variety of managers and employees — enforcing only one strict rule: The vision statement could be no longer than eight words.

The statement says simply, "Caring now for the future of life."

To Sheng, using a vision statement was merely a common sense approach. "Why does the zoo exist? We're here because we care about the future of life, about sustainability," she says. "It points to the programs we are involved in; it points to how we craft exhibits and our education programs. It also points to customer service."

Sheng and her managers have been able to develop a number of mission statements for different operations that use the vision statement as a starting point. The result: a better focused, more effective organization armed to cope with change.

Establishing a values system that helps bring meaning to the workplace has become fairly commonplace in the private sector. So have discussions of giving employees more responsibility so they can help improve an organization's performance. But public-sector managers usually rely on more traditional, hierarchical, techniques.

Whether public sector or private, what holds true for a CEO holds true for other managers, too. In order to do your job well, you have to start with three broad goals:

- To create vision and mission statements that define your purpose;
- To communicate these statements clearly and effectively; and
- To measure and encourage progress.

If you accomplish these three goals, you've gone a long way toward realizing a fourth: To build a culture that makes your company a good place to work — and thus improves your prospects for success. You need to give your company a strong sense of purpose.

Achieve all of this and you'll take control of your dreams. You'll be living your vision.

Bridging Vision and Mission

We begin to bridge the gap between business plan and game plan by considering a company's vision statement and mission statement. Vision and mission statements are different things — but closely related.

The vision statement expresses what the company wants to be in the business world. The mission statement expresses what the company does to achieve its vision. The vision statement expresses the end; the mission statement, the means. The vision statement sets the goal. The mission statement tells you and your employees what to do in order to reach that goal.

A simple statement of goals

When Richard Haworth succeeded his father as president of Michigan-based Haworth, Inc. in 1976, one of the first things he did was create a mission statement, called "The Haworth Creed," summarizing the company's standards and goals.

At the time, the manufacturer of office furniture had 250 employees and $14 million in annual sales. By 1994, the company had 7,000 employees worldwide and annual sales of more than $800 million.

In 1993, Haworth introduced a revised statement called "Our Principles," modernizing and simplifying the language so that it is more readily understood around the globe.

The Principles included a vision statement which clearly articulated the company's long-term goals. It's a simple, 21-word announcement:

> *Our vision is to be world class in the eyes of our customers at creating well-designed, effective and exciting work environments.*

Haworth's mission statement involves more explanation. As do most effective mission statements, it describes the most likely means by which the company can realize its vision.

> *Haworth competes enthusiastically in a free enterprise system. Our style is aggressive and our practices honest; our conduct is legal and ethical. We are motivated by a fair return on investment and are committed to strengthening the company through reinvestment. We believe that customers will be attracted by what we offer and this will ensure our continued success.*

> *To completely satisfy our customers is our primary mission. We listen to our customers and understand their changing needs. We achieve their satisfaction by quickly translating their needs into products and services that are world class and that emphasize quality, design, innovation, and value. We are convinced that the success of our business depends on satisfied customers. . . .*

> *Haworth members [employees] are the most important resource of our company. The diver-*

sity of their races, genders, talents and personalities enables us to be more innovative, dynamic, and flexible. Our members endorse the practice of continuous improvement, believing it offers the best path to pride in their work, greater job security, customer satisfaction and success for our company. Our corporate culture offers a participative environment that supports teams and individuals. Haworth encourages member development and achievement through recognition, rewards and opportunities for career growth.

In order to achieve total customer satisfaction, Haworth methods of operation are shaped by our dedication to quality. Corporate-wide quality initiatives result in superior products and services for our customers. At Haworth we combine smart thinking with hard work to eliminate wasted time, effort and materials. . . . Our philosophy of quality includes the preservation of our environment and the protection of resources. Our pursuit of quality extends to our communities, where we build for the future by investing in the quality of life.

For Haworth, the results have been positive. In 1994, the company announced that it would build a new manufacturing plant in the Ludington, Michigan, area. The 90,000-square-foot plant would employ about 60 people initially and as many as 100 over time. A number of other cities wanted to attract the plant — but Haworth felt staying close its corporate home did the most to advance its mission statement.

"Most people are too close to their own situation to look objectively at what they ought to be going for. A small business operator can have a great idea, but cannot see the land mines ahead," warns Jim Morehouse, with Chicago-based consulting firm A.T. Kearny. "A wonderful entrepreneur can have great vision, but be blinded by the obstacles. Good mission and vision statements will keep them focused."

What to do today

Practical Matters

Many owners and managers feel that a mission statement is the best tool for getting everyone in the company going in the same direction. Just as important, developing a new or revised mission statement forces managers to think tactically.

The main goal: To avoid getting so busy managing today's business that tomorrow's gets pushed aside. Goals are most useful when they help you decide what you and other employees should be doing at work today to help you achieve what you want for the future.

This forward-looking perspective is complicated by the fact that only after a company has done some business can an owner or manager make a useful assessment about work challenges and how a company should respond. It's only after people have purchased your product that you'll find out who your market really is — rather than who you thought it would be.

Business Customers

Blazing Graphics, a Rhode Island-based graphics production company, has developed an elaborate mission statement that proposes to provide all visual services for business customers. The company has revenues of approximately $8 million and 80 full-time employees.

Rick Trahan, vice president at Blazing Graphics, says that by putting all printing disciplines under one roof, the company could increase efficiency as well as a offer a better product. Departments could communicate and work efficiently through any job. The vision: quick delivery, high quality, low cost — for everyone to benefit.

Blazing Graphics' current mission statement, written in 1992, came out of its business plan. "We adapted a Total Quality Management approach," says Trahan. "The game plan is an evolving process.

What we're doing may change. You have to keep the company dynamic."

The mission statement reads:

Blazing Graphics will provide you with the most effective visual communication attainable. We will help you achieve all of your goals while providing you with the greatest value both seen and unseen.

Here at Blazing Graphics we will take the time to do things right. We do this by controlling the entire graphic arts process. This enables us to better coordinate each job while providing a higher level of service. Our mission is to ensure exceptional quality by opening up communication between crafts normally separated and at times adverse to one another.

Here at Blazing Graphics we have committed ourselves and our resources to being on the forefront of technology.

Creative technical know-how is the single most critical determinant of economic competitiveness.

It's our real belief that together we can create an environment that will be both personally and professionally fulfilling for all the people who make up the Blazing Community.

Trahan says the key measure for the company is profit or loss in a given quarter. "We're still sort of new at this. Our neighborhood is very competitive. The market's been changing. And technology is very expensive. So far, banks look at ratios . . . quarter to quarter. And we are profitable."

Although they affect the bottom line, "mission statements are never about bottom line goals," CEO Alan Blazar says. "Profit is not a value around which employees are likely to rally." Instead, a mission statement should incorporate values that are worthy of your employees' best efforts.

In order to monitor performance, a computer system designed especially for the printing business tracks billable hours, materials used and the types

Worthy of your employees' best efforts

of jobs undertaken. The system maintains revenue by department — it's the company's main control device.

The average Blazing Graphics employee bills about 70 percent of his or her hours. "We're hoping to get that number up around 80 or 85 percent," says Trahan. The company's mission statement, with its emphasis on a strong commitment to quality in the workplace, has gone a long way in helping attain that goal.

SWOT Analysis

An approach to bridging vision and mission, which has gained popularity in the early 1990s, is so-called "SWOT Analysis." SWOT stands for Strengths, Weaknesses, Opportunities and Threats. The system stresses a more complete perspective on what accounts for success in a company. It was developed by the Massachusetts-based Boston Consulting Group in the early 1970s.

SWOT Analysis is a graphic thing. It clearly maps out particular — and sometimes recurring — aspects of a company in a consistent manner. It makes disparate steps and activities easy to compare. For this reason alone, many managers use SWOT on at least an occasional basis.

Advocates say that SWOT Analysis works well because it contrasts the internal and external factors that affect a company. They argue that it matches the strengths found in the company's internal environment with opportunities in the organization's external environment in a way that makes performance standards self-evident.

Scanning the internal environment includes an analysis of the company's structure, its culture and its resources. The following areas should be considered in SWOT Analysis:

- The formal and informal organizational structure of the company (number of management levels, span of control, departmental interaction)
- Clarity of communications

- The factors influencing management activity and the goal setting process

- Application of standards of performance

- Management, technical, and professional staffs (education, experience, apparent and demonstrated skills, flexibility, potential)

- Current work force (skills, turnover, absenteeism, experience, labor/management relations)

- Availability, quality, nature and degree of employee involvement

- Professional and labor talent pool in the surrounding area

- External constraints (regulatory politics, market condition, capital availability).

When you've identified strengths, weaknesses, opportunities and threats, you can compare each to your vision and mission statements. Does your SWOT profile match your goals? If there are illogical connections or inconsistencies, what do they mean?

Measuring Progress

Once you have set your vision and mission, you endeavor to set performance standards by determining key success factors, corporate objectives and action plans. Performance standards can accomplish several goals — the most important among these: Monitoring on a regular basis the progress your company makes. Simply said, performance standards serve as yardsticks allowing you to measure how well you do the things that win business. But — like so much else that relates to managing coworkers, customers, vendors and other constituencies — their implementation isn't quite so simple.

Some experts will say that a good business plan defines performance standards by itself. That's not always true. They don't even relate exactly to the quality/value/service triad of market forces. Performance standards have more to do with art of good management than the science of accurate financial projection.

Match your profile to your goals

Stress clarity

Another way to think of performance standards: They're the practical expansion of your company's core competency. Defining them helps you extend what you do well now into what you need to do to meet your goals.

Practicality is the essential aspect of setting performance standards. Realistic goals distinguish a workable business plan from an unworkable one. Most managers find it easiest to break out performance standards along the four primary business functions we've discussed before — Finance, Marketing, Product Development and Operations.

Finance

In many ways, you'll have the easiest time setting up performance standards for your finance department — finance is all about goals and measurement. It's always good to stress clarity, because financial people will sometimes mistake intricacy for completeness.

You do well to focus on the traditional performance parameters that most companies have to meet — unit cost, return on investment, cash flow and profit margin. The challenge in setting financial objectives often has less to do with numbers you target than with translating those numbers to your co-workers. You want everyone in your company to understand cost-basis and cash flow, to say — or at least think: "I sold x plus 20 percent. My costs were y minus 3 percent. My cash flow is greater than I thought it would be."

Sometimes it's necessary to refine your financial perspective: to adjust a product line, eliminate low-volume or -margin products, or restructure operations. In these cases, you can set particular goals that your finance people have to meet.

The regular revision of financial objectives sets up a level of discipline. You should monitor financial performance as close to real time as you can. Monthly is good — weekly is better.

Marketing

Marketing is about information. Marketing performance standards should give you useful information about your industry sector, your competition, services you need to provide, relevant customer demographics, and anything else that relates to what you make and how you make it.

In marketing circles, experts talk about the six P's: product, price, packaging, purchasing trends, public response and profitability. You should make sure that your standards include the tracking of practical information.

Some managers (especially at smaller companies) make the mistake of thinking of marketing as a process that stops when the actual selling of a product begins. While your marketing department may play a bigger role in the early part of a product's life cycle, it should provide you with information throughout. Your marketing department should serve as a early-warning system for changes in your business.

Product Development

Good performance standards add a variety of strengths at a product's inception. They should allow you to think about the future in terms of the other three main business functions. How will you market and sell the product? How much money will it cost — and generate? What will you have to change internally to make the product?

Product development standards should offer you a fresh perspective on your business each time you start a new project. You can reconsider your customer requirements. You can review your design and manufacturing standards.

During any assessment of new products, you're likely to find a number of potential improvements to operations and other functions. This is the reason so many owners and managers like to be involved in product development — it's where the most innovative thinking goes on.

The arena of creative thinking

27

A fail-safe test

One performance standard should be to evaluate all the new ideas to determine their immediate and long-term value. You may want to test the ones that have high immediate value and won't limit other options that may be implemented. Longer term improvements that require enhancing or replacing any significant assets will probably not have as high a priority as improvements that have an immediate positive impact on the mission.

Operations

The purpose of performance standards for operations is to get higher-quality products to market faster and at a lower cost than your competitors can. And you should think of your own historical performance as a competitor.

Basically, you need to determine what levels of capacity, capability, and performance (and what — if any — changes in policy, procedures and practices) you need from operations to reach company-wide goals. Some specific examples:

- How much equipment, process capacity and facility space is needed?

- Where should this design, equipment, process capacity and facility space be located?

- How many and what kind of people are needed in each function?

- What kinds of design, management information and control, materials and resources and distribution systems are needed to support your projections?

- Do your operating policies, procedures and practices support the plan?

Operations standards act as a kind of fail-safe test of broader goals. If the cost of providing or correcting these resources exceeds the practical limits set up in your budget, you'll have to prioritize your company-wide goals and make decisions about which goals you can realistically meet. Or, on the other hand, where you're willing exceed your limits to meet your goals.

In the early 1990s, Emery Worldwide Inc. was losing nearly a million dollars a day. The company had not turned a profit since 1985. It's problem: It had strayed away from its original focus and tried to become a full-service shipping company. By 1994, with refined and clearly-communicated performance standards, the airfreight carrier turned its past performance around.

Emery president and CEO Roger Curry said four steps led Emery to profitability. The first was communicating its business plan's marketing and operations goals to employees and the marketplace in general.

Curry stressed the importance of the company's mission statement by repeating it like a company mantra:

We are an airfreight company . . . providing time-definite transportation services to handle our customers' parcel, package and freight shipments 5 pounds and up around the world.

Part of articulating that mission statement was proving to Emery staff that management would stick with it to provide a foundation for the corporate culture. The company had lost its focus through several ownership and management changes.

The second step stemmed from the first. Once it had communicated the mission statement, Emery had to get down to the business of reshaping itself. "We had to reconfigure operations to improve our service and efficiency, with vigilance on cost control," Curry says. "As part of that plan, we de-emphasized the envelope business, in which we had only a modest market share at best.

International Operations

Emery's international operations generate about one-third of the company's total revenues. It operates in 88 countries, with 1,300 employees and about 150 offices divided among four international sectors. Many of the company's best customers operated globally and were looking for one company that could manage all elements of the supply chain.

Four key success factors

Direct stake in the outcome

To satisfy them, Emery introduced Logistics Worldwide, an international multi-modal logistics and information service. The airfreight carrier's foundation for such a service was already in place.

The next step was to get employees excited and give them the confidence they needed to "Make Emery a Great Company," as the company's internal publicity exhorted. Marketing plans and strategic goals were communicated throughout the company, with simplified projections posted in central facilities. Management spent six months concentrating on making the new focus known to everyone from mid-level managers to entry-level freight handlers.

The final step was to give employees a direct stake in the business improvements. Non-union employees received an incentive compensation plan to share in the airfreight carrier's profits from 1993.

The strategy worked. In the second quarter of 1993, Emery led other domestic carriers in market share for packages over 70 pounds. It controlled 19 percent of the domestic overnight shipping business and 8.5 percent of exports in the heavier weight classification. In total U.S. export market share, Emery's 7.2 percent was second only to Federal Express's 14.4 percent.

Key Success Factors

In any monitoring process there are hundreds of measurable parameters. You need to define and track the business factors that are most important to the customer and most essential to your core competency.

In most cases, you do well to consider every process as a series of set check points or benchmarks. What specific things do you have to do well to accomplish a specific end — to develop a new product? To make that product? To sell it? To ship it?

When you've determined the necessary activities that go into each step in your business process, take a step back and ask three important questions. Do your customers value these things? How do you use your assets to accomplish these things? And how do you measure performance?

The answers to these various questions will lead you from the general concept of performance standards to something more specific: key success factors.

For many manufacturers, the ratio of orders to cash is a key success factor. This tells them how likely they are to meet a specific order in a given amount of time. Other companies use projected revenue-per-employee ratios or inventory turnover as key factors. Beginning in the late 1980s, American car makers put a lot of emphasis on new product realization. That's a key success factor, too.

Less Objective Factors

Other companies — usually service-oriented ones — emphasize less objective factors.

EMCON is a California-based engineering and consulting firm specializing in waste management and environmental compliance issues. The company has 1,200 employees scattered across country and revenues of $98.6 million in 1993.

In an industry sector that has undergone massive changes over the last ten years, the company needs to have a strong, consistent sense of direction to distinguish itself from scores of competitors who will do anything they have to in order to generate fees. Though the company was founded in the mid-1970s, it wrote its first mission statement in early 1990s.

In the past, the company's "business plan tactics didn't necessarily support strategies — or if they did, it was by coincidence. Now, our business plans support our mission statement," says president and CEO James Felker. "A business plan is the first stage of implementation of the mission statement . . . and success factors."

His mission statement reads:

> *EMCON's mission is to provide superior environmental consulting, engineering, and laboratory services as a national, full-service company. We strive to meet these goals through the deployment of a Total Quality Management Program.*

The next step: the action plan

Our highly trained, skilled and dedicated professional staff, located strategically throughout the country, are focused on customer service and motivated to exceed client expectations. Our goal for all projects is high quality service, on budget, and on time, every time.

We are a professional services business, driven by the needs and demands of the marketplace, and we maintain a flexible, resourceful ability to respond effectively and successfully to market changes and opportunities.

At EMCON, our employees are the foundation of our success. We aspire to cultivate a spirit of teamwork and to create a rewarding and challenging place to work.

In 1993, the company was able to reduce manpower structure by 9 percent and raise revenues almost 4 percent, because it had made high revenue-per-employee a key success factor.

Looking forward five years, Felker wants EMCON to be approaching $200 million in sales. That's essentially doubling its size with a commensurate growth in earnings per share.

He says that the success factor for achieving that objective is the development of "seamless information technology networks" throughout the company. Management will measure this in terms of response time of various field offices to information or service requests.

Narrowing Focus

Listing your corporate objectives narrows things even further. Here you answer the question: "What do we have to do — and when — to capitalize on our key success factors?" If, for example, you consider customer-responsiveness a key success factor, you might conclude that your marketing department needs to survey your customers on this subject a couple of times a year. If you consider finding and retaining high value customers a key success factor, you might direct your accounting and sales departments to analyze your best current customers and how you sell to them.

Once you decide what to do, you have to decide who does the work — and this takes you to the action plan. Here you break down the workload by department, team and individual. You let each one know what part it plays in the overall plan, when it must complete a given task and how it can measure its own success.

Maine-based Lepage Bakeries is one of New England's biggest commercial baking operations. The company uses its vision statement as part of an integrated system of continuing improvement and quality goals.

"We weren't a company attempting to right an ill by bringing in a new system of communication management," says chairman Albert Lepage. "We discovered that many of the things we were doing already were MTQ."

MTQ—an acronym for "Managing Total Quality"—influences much of the company's operations. It helped develop a vision statement, which the bakery's executive management group hammered out during a company retreat in the fall of 1992. The statement articulates in plain language where the managers wanted the company to be:

> The Lepage Bakeries' vision is to be the most consistent, productive and respected baking company, to exceed customer expectations and to provide an ever-increasing economic opportunity for all of those associated with Lepage Bakeries.

Once this vision had been defined, Lepage Bakeries had to get to the difficult business of communicating it to employees spread throughout Maine and New Hampshire. They began by using the vision as the basis for a strategic quality statement:

> All associated with the bakery shall be honest, sincere, willing to learn. All shall cooperate, communicate and work as a team to help Lepage Bakeries achieve its vision.

Making good on the vision statement

Do the footwork

An Explicit Connection

This quality statement simply made explicit the connection between the vision and each employee's role in its implementation. It became the company's main tool for communicating its vision.

Next, the bakery's executives created a list of projects on which teams of employees from a cross-section of the company could work to implement the vision. From this list, the executives selected what they thought were the three most critical projects to attack within the first year of the quality-management process. The projects were:

- Formalizing consistent performance evaluations throughout all facilities;

- Reducing defective products; and

- Developing at least one new product using existing facilities and equipment.

Albert Lepage says the projects serve a variety of purposes simultaneously. They streamline troublesome functions, bring together people from disparate ends of the company and — most importantly — give employees comprehensible objectives through which to understand the company's vision.

By late 1993, the company had extensive plans from each of the teams assigned to the projects. By early 1994, it had substantially completed all three.

Communicating What You See

"You must get your viewpoint across clearly and concisely," says Donald Kuratko, the Stoops Professor of Business at Ball State University. "If the vision statement is clear and concise, then it will be easier to convey to buyers, employees and the rest. Get out. Do the footwork. Touch the marketplace."

Of course, the best way to lead is to take your vision and mission statements seriously yourself. If you provide a living example, other people will follow. You must concentrate on the issues of employee motivation and the vision statement. If you have a clear vision statement and a motivated work force, the numbers will go a long way toward taking care of themselves.

The three factors that influence a company's sense of itself relative to its market and competitors are quality, value and service. When you set the terms that will define your sense of purpose, you have to find some balance among these three forces.

People usually go into business because they have some particular idea about a thing they can make or a service they can provide. So, you may think you've defined your product or service well — but you still should reconsider your focus on a regular basis.

Defining your product is less a matter of what you think you should be doing; it's more a matter of anticipating what your customers will think you should be doing.

The management process you use to develop and implement a business plan will affect the quality of the results you achieve. In the traditional mode of planning, a central group formulates strategy for management that is later issued to line personnel. This method of planning and implementation originates in a vacuum and communicates through inefficient channels. All too often, it leads to misunderstandings, frustrations, and lack of support from the personnel who are expected to carry out the strategy. They feel no responsibility or sense of ownership for the plan or results since they had no involvement in the planning process. In the modern economy, no company can afford this level of detachment.

The Right Environment

The best alternative is a more participative approach. This involves cross-functional teams of empowered line management and staff specialists in the development of functional strategies. The specialists may be employees, consultants, or a combination of both. Such participative approaches are

The defining moment

more likely to generate the understanding, patience, and support you need to implement your business plan successfully.

Paul Giddens, manager of human resources planning for Ohio-based General Electric Aircraft Engines, says business and industry have to nurture "the environment where people can contribute to the limits of their abilities and get the motivation to improve their competence."

Giddens says that owners and managers have to start thinking like the Wizard of Oz. In that story, Giddens reminds managers, "the wizard, who is a phony, gives the scarecrow a diploma [and says] 'Now go act like you're smart.' He has been smart all along."

Likewise, a manager can't actually empower workers. But that manager can pursuade them to use the power within themselves. Some management consultants refer to this kind of exceptional effort as a "defining moment." They'll tell you that defining moments are contagious. When one employee exhibits exceptional commitment, others will follow. Your mission statement tells them where to channel that commitment.

When a coworker makes an exceptional effort to do something right or fix something that's wrong, you have a good indicator that your mission statement works.

A 1991 survey of line managers taken by *Industry Week* magazine and the Wyatt Co., an Illinois-based management consulting firm, supported the practicality of employee empowerment. Of the respondents from companies with explicit programs dedicated to employee involvement in management decisions, 76 percent reported improved quality, 73 percent increased productivity and 59 percent increased profitability.

A Hesitant Start

Douglas Smith, the president of Kraft General Foods Canada Inc., had problems initially implementing a customer-focused quality program in his organization.

"Our first attempt started with·quality training for the senior management team. The training they received was then cascaded down into the organization through training teams that we formed to address various tasks," he says. "We measured and tracked the number of teams, the number of facilitators, the number of people trained. A year later, the organization was essentially unchanged."

Why did these efforts fail? Smith concluded that his vision of quality wasn't part of the fabric of the organization. The executive team members hadn't changed their own behavior to achieve higher quality — so, neither had the employees. The vision hadn't become a way of life for people at KGFC.

One of the reasons: What KGFC originally called its vision statement was 65 pages long. It was a complete game plan — including a corporate history, a study of core competence[1] and a SWOT analysis.

This was all great stuff — but it was too much. A classic vision statement has several characteristics: it is clear, understandable and aligned with the company's values; it involves people throughout the organization; it is memorable; it is linked to customer needs; and it requires the organization to work hard to obtain its goals.

By 1992, Smith had reshaped KGFC's vision statement into a more-traditional 46 words:

> *Our vision is that by 1996, we will be recognized as a leading food company in the world and will meet the needs of Canadians. By so doing, we will be known for consistently meeting or exceeding our various commitments and achieving consistently superior financial results.*

In implementing this new vision, Smith learned two distinct lessons. First, he came to understand the importance of making the company's strategy concrete and deploying it to everyone in the company. The vision couldn't be an abstraction understood only by a few people at the top of the organization. Second, he realized the importance of using what he calls "policy deployment" to help employees understand and pursue the company's vision.

---

[1]See page 51 for more on core competences.

A detailed focus

Key Strength

As KGFC defines it, "policy deployment" combines the assertion of corporate objectives and detailed focus of performance standards. In fact, a key strength of KGFC's second effort at implementing quality improvement was its recognition of six "competitively unique capabilities" (strengths) that every employee could help develop:

1) The company's superior value brands

2) The ability to adapt quickly

3) A goal of world-class manufacturing

4) Effective consumer responsiveness

5) Good use of information technology

6) Development of a constructive organizational climate.

Next, KGFC identified performance standards — specific things that have to happen within a year if the six capabilities were to be fully realized. Smith and his managers created a timetable, assigned responsibilities and developed measurements of quality, cost and delivery.

The performance standards became departmental goals. Senior managers changed the way in which they interacted and communicated with line managers and workers. "We tried to begin to live quality," Smith says. "A quality effort needs to be implemented by everyone in the organization. No matter what strategy an organization chooses, success ultimately depends on whether people change their actions."

A Fundamental Impact

When you've set the basic objectives you need to run a company efficiently, you'll usually find you've done a lot more work than you realized.

These tools don't always come easily to entrepreneurial managers. You might doubt the value of something as abstract as a vision statement. But give the matter a chance — exercises that seem simplistic to you may have a fundamental impact on your employees or customers.

Long-term improvements usually depend on fundamental managerial and engineering changes. These things take time to develop and implement. In the case of new companies, birth pangs confuse most owners and managers. In the case of older companies, inertia that has accumulated over years can't be overcome easily. But, by all standards, this is a steady start. It's a start that you can implement.

You need to think of your business as a process in which every person involved plays an indispensable role — or they don't exist. And this process is ongoing, as long as your company is in business. It's not over when your salespeople sign a customer. It's not over when you cash that customer's check. It's not over when you ship your product.

If ever, it's over when the phone rings again, and the same customer places another order. And then the whole process starts once more.

Putting It In Writing

Developing a consistent strategy helped turn around North Carolina-based Healthtex, Inc., a children's-clothing company that had gone through some significant ownership changes through the 1970s and 1980s. Starting in 1991, Healthtex president and CEO Gary Simmons and his management team decided they needed to put in writing what Healthtex wanted to do and who its target customers were.

The vision statement devised by Healthtex is so short that management printed it on plastic cards that employees could easily carry in their wallets. The statement reads:

Healthtex will be the most responsive kidswear company in understanding and meeting the needs of targeted consumers and retailers with basic and . . . fashion everyday playwear that lasts.

Know your customer

The company identified its primary customer as a mother of children, newborn to six years old, who shops for everyday playwear in middle-market department stores and national children's specialty chains.

"We now are a profitable company and are now moving forward very nicely," Simmons says. The statement has helped by getting different groups of people within the company to focus on a strategic direction. "The goal here is that everybody — be it a machine operator, a designer, or the head of human resources — is thinking in a similar vein. It doesn't mean they all think alike, but at least they all have a central core belief of what this company's trying to achieve."

Simmons says he tries to limit the number of goals he sets for the company at any given time. "Fifteen goals take people away from the major mission," he says. "We have three to five instead — all team-based goals we try to accomplish on a yearly basis."

In addition, Healthtex has six performance benchmarks that it calls "gold standards." These include:

- Profit margin
- Operating profit
- Sales and general administrative costs
- Cost of capital
- Bottom line profit
- Return on assets

Simmons and his senior managers set specific numbers as targets for each ratio each year. "If you achieve all these, you've done well," he says.

And Healthtex has. It's experienced 40 percent growth in each of the past two years, and its annual sales increased from $100 million to $150 million.

When you've finished working through the exercises in this chapter, you should have a good idea of the best practical goals you can set for your company. You should be able to look toward the horizon without tripping over any obstacles at your feet.

Vision Statement

Vision is what a leader gives his or her followers. It is his challenge to himself and to the world. It's something worth doing. It's the match that lights the fire of potential in people. It keeps a company on track in good times and bad.

To have a purpose and communicate it defines leadership. This is the statement of your decision to act, and a definition for what direction that action will take. You cannot lead a group of people unless you set a direction.

A vision statement uses the future to help analyze the present. As the head of your operation, you have to articulate the blend of present and future. Expressing corporate purpose is the most important task management has.

A company needs a vision statement that everyone from the CEO to the receptionist can understand. It formulates what an organization wants to be and stimulates specific goals that can be passed down to every department in the organization. It needs to be something useful and applicable to daily operations. You — and, more importantly, your co-workers — should feel comfortable using your vision statement in everyday conversation.

What does your company do? Why does it do that? In a world where advances in automation and productivity have transformed many traditional value-added businesses into commodities, successful companies need a strong sense of purpose.

Although you are excited about your new vision, you see it clearly, and you're motivated to change your organization, you still have to make your coworkers feel the same way that you do.

Vision means something to people at all levels in an organization. Lower-level employees might not know the specifics of the company's marketing plans or financial outlook, but they do know its reputation. They know how other players in the industry or local market perceive it. They know when they

Vision Statement

When you started your company, what did you see it becoming in ten years?

What is your purpose?

What do you want to be the best at?

Drafts of your vision statement:

_____

_____

_____

_____

_____

_____

_____

Taking Control Series Form # 1
1994 © The Merritt Company

work for a quality-driven organization, or one that's content to skim margins from second- or third-rate work.

If you build an environment that values quality, in which people can be proud of their efforts, you'll find better people more easily. And you'll be able to keep them once you've found them. But you can't achieve quality without explicitly saying you want to achieve it. It isn't something people infer from all companies. It isn't something you can receive passively. You have to set it up as a goal and pursue it continuously.

Something you'll find as you do this: People — employees, vendors, customers — want to believe in quality. It's rare enough that it has intrinsic value. People will work hard when they understand a vision that seeks quality performance. That kind of vision empowers people to perform well.

Results come when people develop a shared vision of how they want their organization to be perceived and are willing to work every day to maintain that vision.

Sam Walton had a vision for Wal-Mart. He believed that giving median to low-end retail customers in smaller geographic markets the widest possible choice of inexpensive goods would establish his chain as the market leader among discount department stores.

For McDonald's, Ray Kroc believed that cleanliness and consistency more than compensated for the unexceptional taste of hamburgers. The goal of the McDonald's chain is that the food in all of its stores — all over the world — tastes exactly the same. And that all the bathrooms are reasonably clean.

What is remarkable is that so many employees at all levels in both these organizations still share the founder's original vision.

Directions

First, spend some time talking with someone close to you about your company and your dreams for it. Why you started it, what you wanted to accomplish, what you want to leave behind.

A vision statement is not easy to write in a sentence or two, but writing it will make it clear to you and meaningful to others.

It must have several elements: it must be long-term, meaningful in a human context, and appeal to a higher purpose.

What do good vision statements have in common? You feel you know the company when you read them. They give the company a human feeling, a personality. They set out what the company values. They often refer to quality of life issues.

Try several drafts of your vision on the next page. Answer the questions. Ask people, particularly your employees, to look at your answers.

Questions to ask

Who are you as a company?

Where do you want to make your mark?

How high do you want to shoot?

What do you believe in?

Does what you have written embody the spirit of where you want your company to head?

Can you live with this vision? Are you willing to (or more appropriately, do you automatically) act in accordance with what you have written your vision to be?

MISSION STATEMENT

A good mission statement gets people to act in agreement with the company's broader goals. It reminds them how to behave every day, regardless of what temporary forces work against them, so that they can help realize the company's vision.

What the vision statement is to strategy, the mission statement is to tactics. It identifies the critical processes that impact implementation of vision. You should have at least one mission statement for your company — and you may develop related ones for each distinct department or division.

The mission of a company is not dreamy, like a vision. It is based in today and reality. It defines specifically your product and your market—who you will sell to and what you will sell. Industrial psychologists and management consultants as diverse as Wikham Skinner and Tom Peters argue that the mission statement represents a crucial conceptual link between the business or corporate strategy and the operating functions.

A complete mission statement clearly and fully describes which factors—and, if necessary, which resources — are most critical to supporting the business strategy. The three factors that most managers consider in terms of their mission: Quality, value and service.

Quality and reliability must be defined in terms of the customer and projected back to determine their impact on engineering and manufacturing. Internal quality benchmarks, as useful as they can be in monitoring operations, don't play so vital a role in developing a mission statement. You have to consider the level and meaning of quality and reliability appropriate to the desired competitive position in the marketplace.

Value can mean lowest manufacturing cost, lowest selling price, or best value when other factors are considered. The first two definitions are fairly objective. Even though many management gurus stress

Mission Statement

What do you sell?

Who do you sell to?

What does your company do better than anyone else?

How does your company rank the importance of quality, value and service?

How do you define each of these based on customer needs and expectations?

How will you do what you do to achieve your vision?

Drafts of your mission statement:

_____

_____

_____

_____

_____

Taking Control Series Form # 2
1994 © The Merritt Company

so-called "best value," that definition tends to be so vague that it's useless.

Service includes more than just the friendliness of the greeting a customer hears when your receptionist picks up the phone. It translates into the degree to which you can devote company resources to the needs of a specific customer — without ignoring all others. As we'll consider later on, this has a lot to do with operations. Service entails manufacturing flexibility and versatility, the ability to produce a large variety of products of various volumes to supply a diverse market. And to do so quickly.

Particular companies consider hundreds of other factors, though in some manner almost all trace back to these basic three.

No organization can succeed by concentrating on any one of these factors to the exclusion of the other two. Your challenge is to balance the resources you apply to each in proportion to priorities based on current situations and future positions.

Management should agree on functional mission statements that identify the operating resources that are critical to support the business strategy. For example, Federal Express must look at its processes that address accurate and effective distribution within 24 hours — collecting all the packages from across the country, centering them in Memphis at midnight for sorting, shipping them out at 3:00 a.m. across the country, and delivering them to places of business by 10:30 a.m.

Federal Express's mission statement is short because it defines the product only. Yet, in defining its product only, it has also defined the market: everybody. The typical company's market is not so broad, so it must be more clearly defined in the mission statement.

While a mission statement can be as simple as defining the product and the market, some companies feel that the way they treat employees and customers is just as important in defining who they are as is the product and market.

Since the late 1980s, the big players in the U.S. automobile industry have focused mission statements on reducing new product realization (the time passing from concept to the cars in the showroom) from 48 months to the twelve months that car makers like Honda can boast. Ford, GM and Chrysler have all raised their quality standards to match their foreign competitors, but they suffer in comparison because they take so long to respond to market demands.

Directions

How you define your product will have much influence on how you approach product development and marketing. If you think you sell cars, then you might not think of yourself as the provider of a moving environment. You might think your customers are simply coming to buy a car. But what would they ask for if a car did not exist? They would want something that could comfortably, safely, and reasonably inexpensively move them from one place to another — anywhere, even difficult to reach locations. Defining your product by solving customer problems is essential.

How you define what you do should be clearly tied in with your company's core competency. Your core competency is the thing that you do best. In my company's case it is taking complex data and translating it into something simple to understand and simple to use. The Nordstrom department store's core competency is in developing a relationship with customers. Accordingly, they define their product as the service their sales associates add to the value of merchandise.

The discussion that can lead to preparing this portion of the mission statement may be the most important part of creating it. To be able to clearly define your market may be a more difficult task than you would think.

Look at your own promotional catalogs to see if all of your products have a similar theme that you can define. Like Domino's Pizza, is your primary product speed? Like Nordstrom, is your primary product quality in terms of service? Or like Apple computer, is your primary product quality in terms of ease of installation and use? Like Wal-Mart, is your primary product low price?

Get a list of your customers and look for their similarities. Is your market who you thought they would be? Can everyone who buys from you be classified as a particular group? Or like Fed Ex, is your market everyone?

Take these preliminary ideas to your employees and see if they agree. Have meetings just to discuss these items. Then test them in the outside world. Circulate your drafts and edit and rewrite them until you feel good about them.

Questions to ask

Would your customers and vendors recognize you in these statements? Would they be pleasantly surprised because they could really buy in to these directions?

Are they directions your customers they would agree with?

Does this give everyone in your company a direction for each day when they walk in the door? Is there any ambiguity in what is most important?

SWOT Analysis

Competitive advantage is usually divided into two kinds: internal and external. The analysis of the internal environment and the external environment comes together in the SWOT (Strengths, Weaknesses, Opportunities and Threats) analysis. The point of this exercise is to match the strengths found in the company's internal environment with opportunities in the organization's external environment.

Companies should employ resources in a manner consistent with the given source of competitive advantage they pursue. Before you can make a decision about reacting to an opportunity or threat, you have to understand your own strengths and weaknesses. And you have to believe that your understanding is valid.

Once a company knows where it's going, it should be able to assess where it is so it can see how far it has to go. The SWOT analysis is a tool for looking internally, at your company's strengths and weaknesses, as well as externally, for the opportunities and threats that come to you from outside.

This is a tool often used for a group discussion by key people and for good feedback to management of how employees view the company. A SWOT analysis can be done for the company as a whole, as well as for various departments. This is how I use the process:

Strengths. Our strengths are our core competencies —those things we do better than any of our competitors or that really tie together all the products we offer in a unique way. What internal structures or expertise do we have that are a special source of pride? This becomes the center for determining what we will do in the future. We want to constantly build on the things we already do particularly well.

Weaknesses. For every thing we visualize clearly or do well, there is something we can't see so clearly or do so well. Some of these weaknesses we can change

SWOT Analysis

Date _____

Strengths	Weaknesses
Opportunities	**Threats**

Taking Control Series Form # 3
1994 © The Merritt Company

— others we can't. Where do we need to build our company? What is holding us back or creating a bottleneck for everyone else? If we choose to spend money or other resources in one direction, what other directions do we forego?

Opportunities. The most difficult thing about opportunity is recognizing it. The old adage about opportunity knocking once does apply in many cases, so we need to see it — and be able to act on it — when it comes. What are our greatest challenges in the changing environment of the industries we serve? How will new technologies help us? What will our customers need in the future that we can supply? What opportunities will open up globally?

Threats. As with weaknesses, there are some threats we can minimize and there are others we can't. We need to do all we can to control the threats we can predict — and prepare for the ones we can't. What outside our control could threaten our existence? How might new technology hurt us? What in the political environment (government) might threaten us? Will ups or downs in the economy hurt us?

Make many copies of this worksheet, give them to key staff members and ask them for their analysis independently. Then ask for all the input brought in from each member of the group in each of the four categories. Write out all ideas on a board in front of the group, and then pick seven to ten of the items in each category that seem best to fit your company. As with many management issues, the challenge for you is to judge well which items under each heading are key and which aren't.

Questions to ask

Are you using your strengths to their fullest capacity? Are they things you could leverage by teaching them to more people to develop more product, market better, or be more efficient?

Do you celebrate what you do well enough?

Why have you chosen to live with your weaknesses? Would eliminating these be painful? Result in difficult staff changes or cultural changes? Are they financially costly to resolve?

What is holding you back from taking the most advantage of your opportunities?

Are your competitors taking better advantage of these than you are?

What can you do immediately to minimize threats?

Do you have plans to minimize the damage if any of these threats becomes a reality?

KEY SUCCESS FACTORS

The purpose here is to answer the question: What are the key things that, if we do them well, will ensure our success as a business? The answers may not be easy or obvious, but, I believe, they are all part of narrowing down the business plan to the vision and then to the mission. This process will eventually lead to implementation.

Business owners set goals and objectives. But are they the goals that will relate to business success? If you know those items that, if done, will make you successful, you can set objectives that will make sure you are on track. Setting objectives without first determining your key success factors may mean you are not setting objectives that relate to the success of your business.

As with mission and vision statements, don't identify and publish key success factors that you're not willing to validate with your own actions. If you say the highest quality products are essential, don't allow your employees to ship products they know and you know don't meet standards.

Many time management books preach that you should always be doing the most important things you have to accomplish. Don't waste precious time on small things. Do first things first. Key success factors are a critical element for deciding what is most important. Imagine that every item accomplished by an employee every day related directly to one of those items you have decided are key for success. Would productivity increase?

Fill in the blanks of the sentence: "If we _____ _____, then we will be successful." (There are spaces in this worksheet for three key factors for each of the business functions — finance, marketing, product development and operations. Add more if you think of them.)

Key Success Factors
For The Upcoming Year We Will
Concentrate Our Efforts In These Areas

Finance

Key Success Factor #_____ If we . . .

_____

_____

_____

then we will be successful.

Key Success Factor #_____ If we . . .

_____

_____

_____

then we will be successful.

Key Success Factor #_____ If we . . .

_____

_____

_____

then we will be successful.

Marketing

Key Success Factor #_____ If we . . .

_____

_____

_____

then we will be successful.

Key Success Factor #_____ If we . . .

_____

_____

_____

then we will be successful.

Key Success Factor #_____ If we . . .

_____

_____

_____

then we will be successful.

Product Development

Key Success Factor #_____ If we . . .

_____

_____

_____

then we will be successful.

Key Success Factor #_____ If we . . .

_____

_____

_____

then we will be successful.

Key Success Factor #_____ If we . . .

_____

_____

_____

then we will be successful.

Operations

Key Success Factor #_____ If we . . .

_____

_____

_____

then we will be successful.

Key Success Factor #_____ If we . . .

_____

_____

_____

then we will be successful.

Key Success Factor #_____ If we . . .

_____

_____

_____

then we will be successful.

These are my company's seven key success factors, by business function:

Finance

- Sell each unit at a profit.
- Continue to reduce overhead costs.

Selling each unit at a profit means controlling costs above the gross margin line (those costs that relate directly to producing the product) and the costs of sales and marketing. Selling each unit at a profit insists that you won't continue to produce products or product lines that aren't adding to the bottom line. This doesn't necessarily mean you will discontinue a struggling new product, but you'll have to consider whether you can cut its production or selling costs to make it worth keeping.

Reducing overhead costs relates to costs in the personnel, facilities, and administrative expense section of your income statement.[2] Most companies make an effort every few years to reduce overhead, particularly when economic times are hard. But when sales are up and the profit picture is good, these expenses tend to creep up. It is important to constantly monitor overhead, and continually keep pressure on to reevaluate these costs on an ongoing basis.

Both of these items are essential to your ability to stay profitable. Even if you accomplish all of your other Key Success Factors, but are unable to do this profitably, you won't be able to stay in business very long.

Marketing

- Find and retain high value customers.
- Create and maintain the highest level of customer satisfaction.

One of the factors critical to your success may be retaining business from your top five or six customers, who account for the majority of your total sales. If no one in the company realizes the impor-

---

[1]See page 51 for more on core competences.

tance of these large accounts, managers may set primary objectives to get new business or focus on overall customer service. If you don't define and communicate the critical elements, your co-workers will not know to design a strategy to make sure they don't leave your top customers to take their business to your competition.

Decide who will likely buy your product, make sure they know it exists, offer them easy ways to purchase it, and make sure they buy again by providing outstanding customer service. If none of your key success factors has to do with serving the customer better, you probably won't be in business very long.

At my company, I want customers to come away with more than they expected. Our business is built on a base that we earned over the course of time we've been in business. Some of our customers have been buying from us for 30 years. Can you imagine the value of a thirty-year customer?

Product Development

- Develop new products that capture the needs of our customers, while keeping current products high quality.

It's also hard to imagine not having the success of your business tied in to continually creating better products, if for no other reason than to give your marketing and sales people something new to sell. Customer expectations about product variety, in terms of products fitting their exact needs, increase every year. The ability of customers to determine where else to buy a similar product increases as well with the increase in communication technologies. You must continually do it better or be prepared to lose business.

Operations

- Get products to market quickly, effectively, and accurately.

- Find and retain high value employees.

Some owners and managers overlook key success factors related to operations. That's a mistake — they're central to profitability. "Operations" includes the whole process of getting your product to the people who want it, from prototype to customers' hands. This means how you process orders, fulfill and ship so that customers get what they wanted the first time and on time.

These processes should be continually improved, just like your product. If the time from prototype to market-ready product is three months, what would you have to do to reduce it to one month? If you currently ship product within five days, what would you have to do to do it within 48 hours? And, most pertinent to this discussion, which of your processes most impact profits and customer satisfaction? These may be your key success factors.

Do you often wonder why an employee is working on one project when it is obvious to you that the project that has been sitting in an in-box for three weeks is the more critical one? Maybe you have not communicated as well as you've thought what is important to you. Key success factors communicate which project to do first. Since they start at the top, everyone knows that what they do relates to what the company as a whole does. Key success factors are not phrases like "we need to be profitable" or "we need to stay ahead of the competition." These words do not relate enough to the purpose of the business, nor do they lead employees in any direction.

In addition to setting and communicating your visions and expectations, assembling the best staff you can is an important challenge. The people you hire and how you treat them says more about your philosophy than any vision statement ever will. Employees are key to your success, and objectives should be set every year regarding better training, increasing benefits, systems of compensation, reviewing performance, etc.

Don't continually improve you products and services and neglect to continually improve your personnel and what you offer them.

As with vision and mission statements, route these forms to key employees and then compare responses to check for anything you might have missed.

Do your key success factors encompass all the important areas of your business? Do they truly represent what would make you successful?

If your competitors were to do the same things, would they be successful?

What percentage of your time (personally) and your company's time is spent on making these things happen? If it isn't most of your time, why not? What else is more important?

Do your employees all know that these factors are critical? What ways do you have of telling them?

Corporate Objectives

Key success factors make it clear what we think we must do to make the business succeed in a general sense. Corporate objectives turn these key success factors into specific items to be accomplished. They should also be written to include specific measurements to know if success has been achieved.

To look at how corporate objectives differ from key success factors, I have taken some of our key success factors and suggested objectives that relate to them.

There is one worksheet for each of the major business functions — finance, marketing, product development and operations.

Finance. *Sell each unit at a profit.* All products must pull their own weight. Traditionally we seem to have very profitable products that are pulled down by others that do not justify themselves. One objective is to look at product modifications to reduce the expense of a given product so that its current sales will be profitable.

Continue to reduce overhead costs. This is an ongoing objective for my company — and most. The lower overhead can be, the better. Overhead items (to be discussed in much detail in the financial section) are necessary, but do not add to the making of the product or the marketing of it.

Our objectives usually include reducing reliance on outside services, looking into more effective ways of using insurance, reduction of office supply use, etc.

Marketing. *Find and retain high value customers.* Each word in this key success factor is meaningful. We are looking for customers but not everyone out there would we want as a customer, even in our target market. The kind of customers we want are high value. They value what we value in our product and our service, and our relationship with them is profitable for us as well as for them. And we not only want to find them, we want to do our best to retain them.

If finding and retaining high-quality customers is important, you might:

- develop methods to get feedback from customers, such as surveys;

- streamline procedures to make it easy to order or return your products;

- consider the quality of your promotional material to determine whether it makes your products easy to order; or

Create and maintain the highest level of customer satisfaction. With this statement we aim to create the highest level of service to our customers. And once created, do what it takes to maintain that service level. Objectives might include: Setting up an on-going customer contact program, focusing on special services for your top ten dollar-volume customers, etc.

Product Development. *Develop new products that capture the needs of our customers.* Objectives in this category might relate to changes in each specific product, and how many new products you intend to create. Deadlines for completion are very important to make sure designers are not continually making something better, but never getting the improved design out to customers.

Operations. *Get products to market quickly, effectively, and accurately.* Objectives will relate to time and quality standards. Time issues must usually be balanced against quality issues. The more specific these objectives can be, the better. You may wish to set goals such as all orders being shipped the same day, or adequate inventory levels to assure backorders do not occur.

Find and retain high value employees. Objectives here relate to hiring in new or strategically important areas, training or letting go of weaker team members, adding to benefits, etc. You may set objectives for dollar volume sales per employee, or setting up a bonus system, etc.

Going back to the same groups you used to help you determine key success factors, ask them to list objectives for each key success factor. Next to the objective, write a short description of how you will know if your mission has been successfully accomplished.

What objectives might you set to achieve a particular key success factor? (Answer this with as many responses as you and your managers can generate. Then prioritize.)

Do your objectives fit the key success factor to which they apply?

What objectives might you set to achieve a particular key success factor?

Are the objectives realistic, within a fairly short time?

If you completed all of the objectives, would you feel you have accomplished that key factor for success?

If you accomplished all objectives under each of the four categories, would you be assured of success as a company?

How quickly can you get from perception of customer need to reality?

Corporate Objectives Worksheet #1
Finance

Key Success Factor # _____

_____
_____
_____

# _____	Objectives	How we will define success
# _____		
# _____		

Key Success Factor # _____

_____
_____
_____

# _____	Objectives	How we will define success
# _____		
# _____		

Key Success Factor # _____

_____
_____
_____

# _____	Objectives	How we will define success
# _____		
# _____		

Corporate Objectives Worksheet #2
Marketing

Key Success Factor # _____

_____
_____
_____

# _____ Objectives	How we will define success
# _____	
# _____	

Key Success Factor # _____

_____
_____
_____

# _____ Objectives	How we will define success
# _____	
# _____	

Key Success Factor # _____

_____
_____
_____

# _____ Objectives	How we will define success
# _____	
# _____	

Corporate Objectives Worksheet #3
Product Development

Key Success Factor # _____

_____

_____

_____

# _____	Objectives	How we will define success
# _____		
# _____		

Key Success Factor # _____

_____

_____

_____

# _____	Objectives	How we will define success
# _____		
# _____		

Key Success Factor # _____

_____

_____

_____

# _____	Objectives	How we will define success
# _____		
# _____		

Taking Control Series Form # 7
1994 © The Merritt Company

Corporate Objectives Worksheet #4
Operations

Key Success Factor # _____

_____
_____
_____

# _____ Objectives	How we will define success
# _____	
# _____	

Key Success Factor # _____

_____
_____
_____

# _____ Objectives	How we will define success
# _____	
# _____	

Key Success Factor # _____

_____
_____
_____

# _____ Objectives	How we will define success
# _____	
# _____	

Action Plans

Once determined, objectives must be set into motion by more specific plans of action, down to the person responsible level, and progress monitored by assigning due dates. Action plans are marching orders and very specific directions for how people need to march — and where they need to arrive at the end of the campaign.

Conceptually, this worksheet is extremely simple. The process applies the theory and abstract concepts that color some of the other worksheets in this section in a practical way.

This is the essence of employee participation in the planning process. Some people enjoy the freedom of a blank piece of paper to dream about what they would like to accomplish. Most, however, just want to know that they can make a contribution.

I try to make it clear exactly what I — and my managers — want this exercise to accomplish. Done well, these action plans can become milestones that we use to gauge performance and progress. That goes for individuals, departments and the company as a whole.

In many cases, this is an appropriate part of a person's annual performance and compensation review. In other cases, we use them on a project-specific basis. Because action plans are so straightforward, they're useful in almost any managerial context.

Give each person who works with you all of the material developed so far (vision, mission, key success factors, and corporate objectives) and then encourage each to write his or her own action plans, linking them to specific corporate objectives.

These action items should be discussed with the manager who set the objectives. They can become part of the employees's personal goals for the year, and compensation decisions can be made using ac-

Action Plans

Person or Team_____

Date _____

Key Success Factor #	Objective #	Action Items	Measurement	Deadline

Taking Control Series Form # 9
1994 © The Merritt Company

complishment of these specific goals as part of the decision process.

There are also objectives within a department or involving more than one department that can only be met with a team of people. Pick the team of people, or ask for volunteers, and give them this worksheet to ask them to develop action items as a group.

Some individuals are much more creative verbally than in writing. Encourage people to sit down with peers from other departments to talk through the meaning of each objective and how their individual work can help contribute. Notes taken from these discussions can translate into meaningful action items.

If you establish this process as a credible exercise, your people will tell you things you might not have even thought of before. And if you can tie a person's paycheck into what you want them to accomplish, and also make sure they are recognized for their achievements by their peers, you can almost be certain that they will meet the objectives that they themselves set.

Once action items are set, negotiate deadlines for completion. Before they are finally written, they should be agreed upon between the manager and the employee, and interim deadlines should be set if it is a long or complex project.

Questions to ask

Do these action items work toward meeting the objective set?

If all the action items under a single objective are met, will the objective be met?

Are these action items clear enough to give employees adequate direction?

Is there any ambiguity about what successful accomplishment means?

Tactical Plan Circle

This is a worksheet to be used explicitly as a communication tool. It translates into graphic form the concepts, objectives and goals you've set out in other exercises.

Pulling together all of the elements from this chapter, we can visually show how each section draws from the previous to make up our tactical plan. It compares different exercises in relation to one another and their overall importance in the management process.

This is a powerful tool for communicating all of the pieces of the planning cycle to your people and for letting them see where their work fits into the whole.

Front-line workers often complain that they're not told where and how their efforts fit into the company as a whole. That feeling can be a major disincentive to effective work and innovation. Take every chance you can to help your co-workers understand their positions in the company.

Colorful eye-catching visual communication is inspiring and exciting. We try to be as creative as we can when we use graphics to represent important business concepts. We've tried a number of different methods — glass jars and beads, toy horses on a track and even old-fashioned thermometer graphs.

But the best way to use a graphic is to compare statistics or trends that don't always leap to mind as relevant but, together, shed insight and understanding on a key business function.

The advantage of this graphic is that it tells everyone where he or she fits in the planning process — usually something companies, especially big ones, keep cramped in the board room.

Taking the information developed from the previous worksheets, enlarge the page that follows until it is large enough to write in, and use it to map out

Tactical Plan Circle

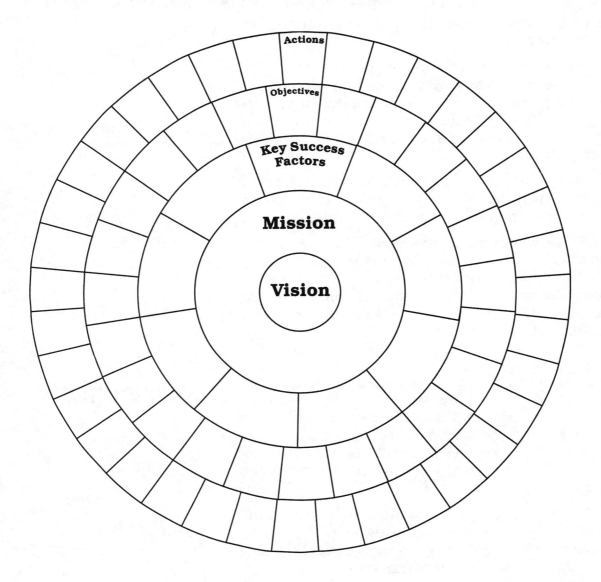

Taking Control Series Form # 10
1994 © The Merritt Company

your tactics for implementation. A wall-sized circle, posted in a common area would be a very effective means of communication on these important areas.

Use your imagination to add color and graphics as appropriate to broadcast your direction to everyone, everyday. Encourage people to study the chart — and even have employees and managers cross off items that have been completed, and date them at company-wide meetings. Celebrate each of these significant events.

Keeping several years of these circles in a conference room will help remind people of how much they have accomplished.

Looking at your circle, do you have a sense of a team pulling in one direction? Do any of the items you see contradict each other?

Does this look like a year's worth of work? Are all of the items significant and meaningful?

Are you excited by the work this represents? Does this circle help you imagine how you will feel when projects are completed?

Questions to ask

CHAPTER 3: SETTING BUDGETS

People hate budgets. You may run your business using your daily bank balance as your only financial tool. Some people do well for years in this manner. But if you don't budget formally, you probably do so informally. You know how much it costs to make your products, and what profit margins you need to pay the bills. And you have a pretty good idea of what your company is worth.

Most people resist the notion that they can benefit from good budgeting — until they try it.

Then they learn that budgeting takes some of the hazard out of business by minimizing the guess-work that comes with winging it. Budgeting gives you a blueprint for action. It tells you what to expect and alerts you to trouble when the unexpected happens. It also measures your success; when your business outperforms your projections, you know you're doing well.

This chapter takes you through the basics of budgeting. It shows you how to put together a "bottom-up" budget — that is, an overall budget that reflects the real needs of your business. It presents case studies that show the value of budgeting to a young business and to the business facing a crisis. The worksheets in this chapter show you how to analyze your average selling prices, your month-to-month unit sales, your sales projections, your payroll, your expenses and your overall performance.

The Basics

Profits aren't everything in business; your vision statement says nothing about profits. But without profits, no business survives long enough to reach its goals.

Fittingly, therefore, almost everything in budgeting stems from the simple formula for determining profit:

The hazards of winging it

A tool for managers

Sales minus expenses. This formula drives business. Profit defines performance, in other words. Everything else is elaboration.

But you prepare budgets *after* you set direction with your vision and mission statements. Like those items, the budget helps to get you from the generalities of your business plan to the specifics of day to day operations. By setting priorities, the budget makes clear what your finances permit you to do to reach your goals. It translates the vision and mission statements into action. As such it speaks more loudly than words when it comes to separating the important from the unimportant, since it specifies action.

Above all, the budget is a tool for all managers, not just CEOs. The financials you show your directors and investors don't tell managers what you expect from them and which of their efforts you value most. Your budget does.

Input from Managers

It's an eccentricity of American business that budgets come down from on high, from senior management. The best budgets show the input of managers. They focus on each business function within the company from the bottom up. They reflect the thinking of the people who know best where the company needs to spend money.

Get the input of these people when you put your budgets and projections together. And build some tolerance for variance into your numbers. Your budget stops being accurate the moment you finish it, and when variances occur — and they will — make sure they buy opportunity for your managers to act creatively.

Remember that finance plays both operational and analytic roles. Some business owners become excessively enamored of quantitative analysis — to the detriment of qualitative analysis. This can lead to problems. Occasionally, when a finance department detects a company-wide difficulty, it can make matters worse by forcing its priorities on other units.

Illinois-based consultant James Morehouse offers a good example. When an internal audit finds too many assets tied up in inventory, "out goes a memo telling all unit managers to cut inventory 25 percent in six months," he says. "But only the hot items move out fast. The rest sit there. When it's all over, inventories are down 10 percent, the CFO declares victory — and the only items left are the ones nobody wants."

Clearly, numbers don't tell the whole story. This leads some entrepreneurs to suspect the value of any process based on detailed guesses projected to points far in the future.

To be sure, projections are guesses at core. Their value depends on the assumptions used at the onset. The better the assumption, the better the projection. They shouldn't go too far into the future, and they should forecast sales conservatively and costs liberally, showing what you might call a constructive pessimism.

Budgets serve as defensive mechanisms against risk, alerting the organization to problems lying ahead by building on the past. The easiest way to begin a projection is to map out at least one year — but no more than three years — based on your performance over the same period in the past. If you don't have that much history, start with the projections you made in your business plan, adjusted to actual performance since you opened for business. If you belong to a trade group, ask it how other members have done relative to their projections. Have they come in over or under their projections? By less than five percent? By more than ten? If you have a specific competitor, try to find out how it has done. If all else fails, find out how businesses in your region do in general.

If you have enough history but show a big spike up or down recently, put it in perspective by going over the numbers for a longer period.

Following the Money

Knowing which of these numbers means the most can yield big benefits, as Andrea Totten discovered

The past projects the future

79

Smoothing out cash flow

in running her California-based quilt-making company, Rags to Riches.

She founded the company in 1971, selling quilts and comforters at flea markets and art fairs, but then used a small catalog to generate orders from stores and designers. "[Business] started getting really busy and that's when I decided that I needed to find a direction," she says. "I guess then I didn't think of the word business plan, but I guess now in retrospect that's what it was."

Totten wrote proposals and went to a variety of lenders only to find most of them reluctant to lend to small businesses and some, it seemed, reluctant to lend to women. "Even though I had a house and a car, they wouldn't take them [as collateral]," she says. "Each year they'd say, 'Come back in a year.' Meanwhile, four or five years passed."

Totten resorted to what she ruefully calls "acid based lending" — high interest loans made against accounts receivable by fashion industry lenders called factors. "You sell your receivables," Totten says. "[The loans] were good at the time because they were needed. But they turned out to be too expensive to maintain."

The factors charged 4.5 percent interest — per month. "The only way to beat it is to keep the money going. And it's like the whole fabric industry is factored. So once the business slows down, it's a killer," she says.

A Heavy Load

She persuaded a bank to lend her working capital when her billings passed half a million dollars. "The bank wasn't that bad, about two percent above prime," she says. Still, Totten found herself devoting 20 percent of her cash flow to servicing debt. And she didn't think her bankers valued small-company business; among other things, they frequently changed the terms of her credit line. She paid her loans down as quickly as she could and eventually got out of debt.

"By the time I took classes on how to write [business plans, the instructors assumed that] you sell

$20,000 and the next month you have $20,000 in because the people always pay on time. Not true. Receivables don't come in that smoothly, and vendors want money. Your labor, of course, is COD," she says. "I brought in $80,000 in cash, where was it? The business plan was hard to keep to because of the fluctuations of our industry."

In the late 1980s, a number of Totten's competitors went out of business. Trouble plagued the retail industry, too. Stores that had always paid their bills on time now stalled her, stretching her receivables out to $10,000 or $15,000. Then suddenly they'd be gone, leaving her with lots of bad debt.

All this led Totten to manage her receivables strictly. "I never let anybody get high enough to ruin me if I lose," she says. "It's kind of like gambling. Don't ever gamble more than you can afford to lose. I look at my receivables and [decide which] people I'll put on COD. If they don't want to buy from me anymore, that's okay because I'm losing money [with them] anyway."

Slow Downsizing

Totten also downsized by attrition, not replacing employees who left. And once she had little or no short-term debt to preoccupy her, she could reassess her market, too. "I said: 'What do I want to do? Do I want to go and look for new business or do I want to better serve the business I have?' And I chose to stay with the stores that were loyal to me and not advertise. I dropped all that."

She was selling to almost 1,000 retailers throughout the country — too many, she thought. She focused on big customers who paid most reliably and cut back doing business with the rest. In the end, she trimmed her customer list by two-thirds but maintained almost the same revenue. "To me, there are two ways to go out of business. One is to have too many orders and the other is to have too few. I used to look at gross sales. But my accountant showed me if I sell $900,000 a year and my profits are higher — that's my success," she says. "Not if I sell a million a year and my profits are down."

She also cut loose her outside sales reps. They took 10 percent commissions and often didn't service the customer well, giving out the wrong information or not knowing the answers to key questions. "So they'd be calling us. I'd be paying two people to do the same job. Now we have our [in-house] reps call and customers fax the orders in. We call back and go over the order with them," she says.

Throughout this restructuring she kept prices steady, protecting her margins. Her strategy translated into stiff terms with her customers. Rags to Riches doesn't give retailers discounts beyond those in its price list — and those only to retailers who display the company's wares prominently.

"It's one thing to get into a new store, but it's another thing to get reorders," she says. In fact, she uses reorder trends as her main diagnostic test for how the company is doing. "If we don't get reorders, then we know that something's wrong. Either the salespeople don't know how to sell [the product] or it's not displayed correctly or it's in the wrong store."

Her final observation about taking control of her company's finances: "Small business people have to keep up with what is happening just as much as a CEO at a huge corporation. If you're not on top of your finances on a real-time basis you're not going to make it."

Controlling Expenses

Andrea Totten grew her business by remaining flexible and by keeping an attentive eye on her market. She controlled expenses and reshaped her finances to fit her needs. She learned the value of understanding the impact of finances on her business.

It's good advice. Evaluate your projections regularly, particularly when adding capital to your business, yours or somebody else's. If you have a hunch about the future, follow it — but look for similar surprises in the past and find out what impact they had; don't adjust your financial projections on instinct. Instead, base your new thinking on as much hard evidence as you can gather. Your hunch may tell you that an upturn lies around the corner — but that new market you pursue may trail the overall economy by a year.

The owners of new businesses often review every expense but, as things progress, they back off. They control expenses with budgets and paper trails—i.e., invoices and purchase orders — and make sure that only a few, accountable people handle cash.

Other points:

Purchasing. In a small business, put one person —not five or six—in charge of ordering merchandise and using overnight mail services.

Supplies. Make your employees aware of the costs of office supplies; some managers mark the individual cost of each item, such as pens, on the box. Hold your managers responsible for expenses in their departments. Keep an eye out for such ancillary costs as delivery fees. You may spend less to send an hourly worker to pick up supplies.

Travel and advertising. Scrutinize expenses such as travel, entertainment, and advertising. Make sure your ads reach your intended market, and monitor the results. Make sure that travel and entertainment expenses pay off with increased business.

Insurance. Ask your carriers about safety programming. Consider increasing deductibles for employee health insurance. When sales and profits are down, tell your carrier. You might be able to adjust your coverage — and premiums.

Records. Maintain good records and paper trails. Most companies that fail don't have adequate bookkeeping and never know where they stand.

A Sharp Point

You pursue two objects in controlling expenses — to eliminate "default spending," or spending by habit, and to set priorities for the spending that you must do. This requires some thinking about the impact of the numbers you study on your business and its future. Sometimes the numbers yield the keys to

Eliminate spending by habit

83

The chance to control quality

keeping a good company afloat, as Florida-based pencil maker Dixon Ticonderoga Co. discovered in the early 1990s.

Dixon Ticonderoga hadn't reported a profit since 1988 and hadn't paid a dividend since 1989. In 1990, losses peaked at $5 million on sales of $82 million. The company makes school and office supply products. Best known for its yellow Ticonderoga pencils, it also sells children's crayons, paints, rubber bands, artist's materials, felt tip markers, and specialty crayons. Unlike its better-capitalized competitors Empire Berol USA and Faber-Castell Corp., Dixon Ticonderoga makes virtually every product it sells. This runs up expenses but allows the company to control quality and scheduling tightly.

CEO Gino Pala considered the situation serious enough to call for a new business plan. He felt the need for deep changes in the way the company did business, particularly in the way it managed assets, structured operations and used budgets.

Pala's team put together a business plan which projected sales and profit out for three years. The effort, he says, stemmed from a question asked by an hourly production worker during a tour of an Ohio plant. The worker asked Pala whether the company would survive its financial problems.

Pala cut middle management and closed two factories. Real estate in Canada and Florida went on the auction block to bolster liquidity. The company established a central R&D lab to shepherd new products to market.

A Key Problem

The company attacked a key problem — liquidity in the first half of its fiscal year. The critical back-to-school season came during the second half; Pala wanted to keep the first half close to breakeven, to maximize second-half profits. He launched a major cost-cutting drive, reducing first-half operating losses by almost 80 percent by the middle of fiscal 1992.

Pala and his managers monitored expenditures directly. They applied cost-evaluation to justify every major bill the company paid; in 1992, Pala says, the company could explain the impact on sales of every payment over $1,000.

The company made a big push into the expanding colored pencils market; its research showed an annual growth rate of 12 to 14 percent in this market. To improve its mastery of inventory and time management, the company started communicating with major customers via computer. It changed its marketing approaches in an effort to address the needs of such mega-stores as Office Depot, Bizmart and other national office wholesalers.

"We identified our key customers — something we hadn't done in a long time," Pala says. "Doing that answered most of our big questions. Once that was done, we knew what we had to look for and what we could just let go. Knowing what's important and what's not is the most important key to writing and using good budgets."

As Pala cut costs, the company looked to expand its market share around the globe. It hired new management for its United Kingdom operations and expanded its ties to a unit in Mexico, yielding "the ability to manufacture labor and energy-intensive items at a significant cost advantage," Pala said.

Dixon Ticonderoga's turnaround efforts paid off. Overall, expenses went down by more than $2 million for fiscal 1992, and the company was on the road to recovery.

Sharing Information

The hourly worker who asked Gino Pala whether Dixon Ticonderoga would survive posed a fundamental question for business owners — whether to share information about company finances, and how much. Progressive managers make it a priority to educate staff on company finances. They make budgets widely accessible, at least within the confines of company facilities.

Still, it scares many managers — even progressive ones — to be open with the financials. As a rule we feel uneasy sharing money matters under any circumstances, considering them wholly personal.

Putting things on paper

And some companies operate in such competitive fields that they risk a great deal if they bandy about their financial information.

But in most companies, you don't endanger your position by sharing at least the most functional financial information with your coworkers. People are sometimes more sophisticated about money than you think; your employees may surprise you with suggestions like the one about inventory that came from one of my hourly employees.[1] In any case they may welcome your openness as a sign of trust. I see sharing financial information as a *quid pro quo*. I expect my employees to give me their best, and in exchange for that, I think they have a right to see how their efforts pay off.

When a new management team took over at Lloyd's of London in January 1993, it promised quick and decisive action to address the insurance giant's life-threatening liquidity problems. Three months later, it released Lloyd's first-ever business plan. It discarded various traditional practices in an effort to restore profitability for investors. If management could do that, it could attract new investors — and desperately-needed capital.

Most importantly, the plan included a regular twice-yearly reporting schedule that would review how implementation proceeded. The reporting mechanism included two key elements. First, it outlined what it called "business plan milestones," which included major accomplishments and the months in which they occured. For example:

April 1993 — Publication of business plan

May 1993 — Legal and Financial Panels established to advise Lloyd's on settlement of disputes

September 1993 — Quarterly Survey confirmed continuing fall in underwriting syndicate expense ratios

October 1993 — First report made to investors on business plan implementation

---

[1]See Introduction

These milestones don't include as many specific financial numbers as most companies would report. Those appear — with considerable explanation and annotation — elsewhere in the reports.

The numbers made up the second key element. As at most companies, Lloyd's management focused on a handful of important ratios. These included:

- The number of underwriting syndicates within the market compared to the total underwriting capacity. Syndicates are groups of investors who actually do the insuring in the Lloyd's system.

- The gross premiums collected. This figure corresponds with a company's revenues.

- The cost per transaction for underwriting syndicates. This figure, which reflects overall operational efficiency, dropped by almost half between 1993 and 1994 when Lloyd's installed a computerized trading and processing system.

These reporting mechanisms give investors in Lloyd's insurance syndicates a good impression of how much business they do and how efficiently they do it. To be sure, the insurance industry has a language and needs of its own. But the overall goal of the Lloyd's reports applies to any company: identify a few important numbers and follow them closely and on a regular basis.

The Bottom Line

You can get away with doing your finances in your head for a while, but when your payroll grows beyond a handful of workers, you need to put things on paper.

Successful companies use their budgeting to identify specific, realistic and quantifiable goals. Budgets bring order to the task of pursuing those goals. First, you identify a revenue or sales objective for the year, using the worksheets in Chapter 2. Then, you identify the tasks necessary to reach that objective. That done, you explore the costs and budget for them, outlining the time and resources you must

Finance carries out policy

Send clear messages

commit in order to reach the goal. The budget quantifies your plan in dollars.

It also tells your managers and employees what you value as an owner or manager. Money sends a clear message about your priorities. Budgets act as a language for communicating your goals to others.

Your budgets send clear messages outside the organization, too. Lenders and investors don't do business with people whose position they can't understand. They want to see budgets for at least a year in advance and often more. They want cash flow projections and a comprehensible plan for making steady profits.

But remember that you don't win when bankers or investors give you money. You win when you pay them off. For new businesses the first order of business is to pay off lenders. The surest way to do this is to identify basic financial factors and measure them, so that you can make mid-course corrections.

It takes work, but don't let financial analysis and reporting bog you down. Finance doesn't set policy except *in extremis*. It carries out policy. If you lock into budgets so strict that you can't make monthly adjustments, bad things are bound to happen.

In short, don't keep your budgets and financial projections in a drawer. Use them to chart the implementation of your strategies. There's no guarantee that careful budgeting and financial analysis will bring the success you want. But you can be pretty sure that without them, failure becomes more likely.

Taking control is a matter of scrutinizing every potential risk that your business faces. That means looking at — and sometimes looking beyond — the bottom line.

USING A BUDGET NOTEBOOK

At our company, we create a Budget Notebook each year that documents every expense item, including which vendors we've used and general ledger numbers to correctly categorize each expense.

The following page represents an index for our budget notebook. The categories in bold type are section topics and have their own dividers. Each line item listed has its own page. Each company will have its own additional items, but these are the main categories that are almost universal.

The importance of documenting your budgeting process cannot be overemphasized:

First, the budgeting exercise in this book makes you really analyze your sales projections and expenses in detail. It doesn't allow you to pass over any item.

Second, it tells your accounting department how you want items categorized for reporting purposes. You may wonder why rents are so high on your reports. It may be because accounting thinks you want equipment rents expense reported here, while you think accounting allocates this expense to repairs and maintenance. This way everyone is clear on which expense goes where.

Third, it will convince your employees, like nothing else, that you mean business about really scrutinizing what is being spent.

I'm convinced that there is only one way to start to review your expenses and project your sales. From the bottom up. And in writing.

Many companies project expenses by increasing each expense item by a regular annual percentage. In contrast, this method forces you essentially to start over each year.

Budget Notebook Index

General Ledger Account Numbers

Sales Projections	
Cost of Goods Sold	
Materials purchased	
Salaries & wages	
Production supplies	
Temporary help	
Shipping supplies	
Mailing & shipping	
Sales & Marketing Expenses	
Salaries	
Sales commissions	
Direct mail	
Advertising	
Publicity	
Consulting	
Other sales & marketing expense	
Overhead Expenses	
Personnel	
Salaries	
Bonuses	
Payroll taxes	
Group life & health insurance	
Workers comp. insurance	
Employee benefit plans	
Officers' salaries	
Employment expense	
Training	
Temporary help	
Facilities	
Rents	
Property tax	
Repairs & maintenance	
Utilities	
Property & liability insurance	
Administration	
Accounting services	
Automobiles	
Bank charges	
Computer supplies	
Contributions	
Depreciation & amortization	
Dues & subscriptions	
Legal services	
Licenses	
Miscellaneous	
Office supplies	
Other professional services	
Retirement plans	
Telephone	
Travel	
Income Taxes	

Taking Control Series Form # 11
1994 © The Merritt Company

This allows you more flexibility to do things like reducing expenses. When you carefully analyze the checks you write, you may find you're paying for things you aren't using. Especially for ongoing commitments such as maintenance agreements, annual review is essential.

Try to use the "miscellaneous" line item as little as possible. I never budget for anything other than petty cash in this category so it will not become a catch-all for items accounting cannot otherwise categorize.

Done well, the budget notebook can be the one place to find all the answers. You can keep copies of contracts in this notebook to show expense commitments you have made for periods of time that may be beyond the current year.

Lastly, this kind of notebook helps employees understand how the company's money is being spent. Employees sometimes overestimate — significantly — how much the owner or manager takes out of a business. They assume that if you take in $3 million in revenue, the owner is taking home $2 million. The notebook shows them how much money it takes to make payroll, pay insurance premiums, pay rent, etc.

Set up your notebook in a three-ring binder first — don't worry about what you'll put in it. Prepare the dividers and have one blank sheet of paper for each item with its title on the top. To begin writing, start with the easiest items first, usually some recurring, consistent expenses. For example, how much do you pay in rent each month? Add to this any information you need regarding your lease, such as the starting and ending dates, and when increases occur. This is a good time to review your lease and look for any hidden costs that will need to be a part of your budget.

Each line item has several general ledger account numbers associated with it. These general ledger numbers are used by your accounting staff to allocate every item for which the company writes checks. By looking at each of the expenditures in each general ledger account number, you can do budgeting from the bottom up. Ask your accounting department to add your general ledger numbers to the right side of this sheet.

The budget notebook starts with sales projections and we focus on them in the first few worksheets. Your sales divider should be followed by the completed Average Price Per Product worksheet, the Unit Sales by Product worksheet, and the Dollar Sales Projections by Product and by Month worksheets. These will give you a system to calculate conservative expectations of sales by which you can realistically budget expenses.

We have four other sections that call for dividers in our notebook:

Cost of Goods Sold—the expenses incurred in making your product;

Sales and Marketing Expenses — what it costs you to sell your product;

Overhead Expenses — most of the other expenses incurred in operating an office; and

Income Taxes — we don't discuss estimating taxes in this book, but you should have a section in your notebook for tax planning, and discuss this with your CPA.

Questions to ask

Are your expense categories all encompassing? Would all of your vendors fit into some category?

Will the categories you have chosen be meaningful in decision making?

Do some of these categories house too many different types of items so it won't be clear to all what the category means?

Average Selling Price per Product

To begin to project your sales for the year, it is essential to know how much you are selling of each unit of product now. This worksheet considers pricing issues, across all of your product lines, in detail.

This is critical if you discount your prices for volume or other criteria. You may think your prices are close to retail, but the average price may be at a deeper discount than they think.

This worksheet is useful in making pricing decisions. In some industries, there are standard discounts and pricing schedules required by retailers from wholesalers.

If you know you must make at least $10 per unit to be profitable, and the discount required by retailers is 50 percent, you must set your retail price at $20 — at least.

The trend in average price per product may also give some important signs about your business and your industry. If the average selling price drops consistently from year to year (as is the case, for example, with computer software), you will have to become much more efficient in production in order to remain profitable.

In addition, this worksheet gives you valuable information about what your customers are willing to pay for your products. This kind of information can be used with the marketing tools we talk about elsewhere in this book. After calculating the average selling price per product, compare this to your largest customers. Are they buying way below this number? Are some of your larger customers willing to buy at a number higher than this?

This approach to determining price per unit may be too basic for companies with complex product lines

Average Selling Price Per Product

☐ **This Year**
☐ **Two Years Ago**

A\nProduct	B\nTotal\n$ Sales	C\n# of\nUnits Sold	D\nSelling Price\n$ Per unit	E\nAverage Price\n$ Per Unit (B ÷ C)	F\n% of Selling\nPrice (E ÷ D)

Taking Control Series Form # 12\n1994 © The Merritt Company

(though the theory behind price per unit measurement remains useful). But it will work in many cases.

To calculate your average price per product, list your products in column A and their total sales volume in column B. In column C list how many units were sold of each. In column D list the selling price for each unit of the product. To compute the average price per unit in column E, divide column B by column C. For F, the average discount from the selling price, divide column E by column D. Complete this exercise for at least two years' worth of information.

Questions to ask

Has your average price per unit decreased or increased over the past two years?

How have your selling prices increased or decreased over the same period of time?

Are discounts — as a percentage — about the same over the last two years or have they stayed the same? Do you have to give up a larger percentage of total revenues over time?

Unit Sales by Product

It is important to begin any series of sales projections with what your actual unit sales were last year. Sales dollars may be increasing year to year because of price increases, while unit volume may actually be decreasing.

The number of things that you sell — regardless of price or terms — reflects the underlying strengths of your business. If unit sales aren't increasing, then you aren't growing in real terms.

Keep the actual numbers that come from these worksheets over time. All products have life-cycles. You will see which products have consistent sales, and which have increasing or decreasing sales. Generally, a handful of products has unit sales much greater than expected (although dollar sales might be right on target, or even below expectations). Most have sales slightly below our usually optimistic projections.

Unit sales are a much better method of measuring real growth than are dollar sales. Dollar sales can be impacted by such things as price changes, and additional charges. Decreasing unit sales provide an early warning signal that can be addressed now rather than later — when dollar volume sales begin to drop as well.

List all the types of products you sold last year in the far left column. Then tabulate the actual number of units you sold for each type of product by month. Add the total units by product in the first shaded column. In the last column, divide this number by 12 to get your average unit sales by month.

Now do this worksheet a second time to project the number of units you expect to sell this year. Project as conservatively as possible. If you do not have a specific reason to expect an increase, use last years' average numbers as a projection. In some products you probably expect a decrease. There will also be

Unit Sales By Product

☐ **Actuals last year** ☐ **Projections for this year** ☐ **Actuals for this year**

PRODUCT	1 Jan.	2 Feb.	3 Mar.	4 April	5 May	6 June	7 July	8 Aug.	9 Sept.	10 Oct.	11 Nov.	12 Dec.	Unit Sales Year-to-date	Avg. Unit Sales by Mo.[1]
Totals														

[1] Divide total year-to-date unit sales by current month number.

Taking Control Series Form # 13
1994 © The Merritt Company

new products to add that you may not have had last year. Factor these differences into your projections.

You can also apply a percentage increase to the number of units sold last year to get a projection for this year, although this tends to be less accurate than estimating what you will sell month-to-month based on marketing efforts.

Finally, this worksheet can be used to monitor how close your actual unit sales are to your projections by adding the actual numbers to a third blank worksheet.

Questions to ask

Are unit sales cyclical as evidenced by sharp increases in certain months or seasons?

Are unit increases due to particular marketing efforts?

Are unit sales obviously affected by particular accounts' buying patterns?

Are new products doing as well as expected as soon as expected?

Have any products sales dwindled during the year or from the past year?

Dollar Sales Projections by Product

This worksheet helps you project, conservatively, the dollar sales using unit projections by product using an average selling price from the prior year.

It is important for the morale of the company to be aggressive in marketing and to have high expectations of the sales growth you want to achieve. But save these proclamations for your sales meetings. The budgeting process considers both sales and expenses. If you project a 20 percent increase in sales for the purpose of determining your profit picture, you may allow yourself to increase your expenses by more than you should.

While the company is busy looking at what it is spending, the sales and marketing people must be busy looking also at what the expected sales are.

Take a very conservative approach to sales projections. Base them as much as possible on what actually happened last year, both in terms of real unit sales and your actual average selling prices. Factor in any price increases and expected unit increases very carefully.

In virtually all but the most disciplined companies, if sales are up, people ease up on the expense reins, and the horse runs free. Almost every employee can find something he or she would like to have to improve his or her lot. If money appears to be no object, people will ask for more than they really need — including everything from office furniture to computer software.

Since the most realistic sales projections are done by looking not at dollars, but at units sold, we begin with the unit sales number from the previous worksheet. The number of units you project will be sold is then multiplied by the average price you got for the

Dollar Sales Projections By Product

A Product	B[1] Unit Sales By Product	C[2] Average Price Per Product	D Projected Price Increases (%)	Projected $ Sales (B x C x D)

[1]From *Unit Sales By Product* worksheet
[2]From *Average Price Per Product* worksheet

Taking Control Series Form # 14
1994 © The Merritt Company

product last year to get an idea of what sales dollars the product would be expected to bring in this year.

It is also important to factor in any price increases, but be very conservative in doing so. If you increase your selling price by 10 percent, often you don't increase your discounted price to high volume purchasers by an equal amount. In this case you might want to only factor in a 5 percent increase in the average price.

To get a total, multiply columns B, C, and D together. The shaded box at bottom should be your total expected dollar sales for the entire year.

Questions to ask

Are projected sales substantially greater or less than actual sales from last year?

Are sales projections particularly aggressive for some products and not for others? Do these differences accurately reflect the positions of various products in their sales cycles?

Are there other significant sources of income not taken into account by product sales (such as shipping and handling)?

DOLLAR SALES PROJECTIONS BY MONTH

This worksheet takes the dollar sales projections developed on the prior worksheet, and allocates them by month by looking at how sales came in by month during the prior year.

Overview

It is important to know when we expect the sales to be booked. For most companies, sales are recorded upon shipment of the company's product.

Directions

Filling in this sheet with your actual sales figures from last year will allow you to see if any of your products are seasonal. Even if sales of your products generally don't appear to have any dramatic fluctuations from month to month, certain products may. This may signal a particular buying segment that orders at a particular time of year. Knowing this may help you spend your marketing dollars for this buying group at the right time.

For the purpose of accurate projections, it is important to do this worksheet twice.

First, use actual numbers from the last full year to get the percentages that are calculated at the bottom of the page. These numbers show what percentage of the total sales was made each month of the previous 12 months. The total in the box at the bottom right should be 100 percent.

List your products in the left-hand column. List your actual dollar sales by product for each of the last twelve months. Total the numbers, month by month at the bottom of the page. Using these total dollar figures, divide the total dollars by month by the total dollars in the shaded box at the bottom right corner. Enter these percentages by month at the bottom of each column.

For your second calculation, use the totals and percentages you just calculated at the bottom of the first Dollar Sales Projections by Product worksheet,

Dollar Sales Projections By Month

☐ **Actuals (last year)**
☐ **Projections (this year)**

Product	Jan.	Feb.	March	April	May	June	July	Aug.	Sept.	Oct.	Nov.	Dec.	Total[1]
Totals	$	$	$	$	$	$	$	$	$	$	$	$	$
% By Month	%	%	%	%	%	%	%	%	%	%	%	%	100%

[1] From *Dollar Sales Projections By Product* worksheet for this year only

Taking Control Series Form # 15
1994 © The Merritt Company

to make sales projections. This time, enter the total dollars by product that you calculated in the previous worksheet (from Dollar Sales Projections by Product) in the far right column, and total at the bottom. Then enter the percentages by month at the bottom of the page from the percentages done on the worksheet showing the actuals from last year. Multiply the number in the total column by the percentage at the bottom to get a number to fill in each box. This will give you an expected dollar sales volume by month.

Illustrating this data graphically (a simple bar chart works well) will increase its impact.

Questions to ask

What effect does seasonality have on sales and cash flow?

How do debt service and other financial commitments coincide with the annual sales cycle?

Will profit margin decrease substantially because of variable costs coming into play during certain times of the year?

Can marketing efforts be adjusted to smooth out erratic cyclical and seasonal sales patterns?

Expense Budgeting

This process gives you a format for writing down and tracking expected expense items, as well as a way to compare last year's expected and actual numbers for the same group of expenses.

This worksheet is an example of what a budget notebook page might look like. I've provided a sample of a page called "rents." "Rents" might include office building leases, parking, warehousing, and equipment rentals. Start by listing, at the bottom of the page, what the budget and actual numbers were for the previous year. This will give you an idea of what the expense figure for this year might be and whether there is a tendency to over- or under-budget for this item.

The "rents" category may include several general ledger accounts — office space rental, equipment rental, warehouse rentals, etc. For each of these general ledger account numbers, your accounting department should have a standard list of vendors to whom they often write checks. Ask to see this standard list on regular basis.

Budgeting should be a participative process. Doing it alone defeats the purpose. Teams should be given the responsibility to analyze last year's bills and project expenditures by category and vendor this year. Especially once you have been through the process a year or two, teams should report to you annually on ways to reduce these expenses, and management's role during the process should be limited to making final decisions on approving expenditures and to putting it all together and to, hopefully, get the desired profit picture.

On each blank sheet first list the type of item, and next to it list the vendor of that item. Lastly, make an estimate of how much you think you will spend on that item this year. This estimate can be made by looking at how much you spent last year and making an educated guess as to whether this will go up or down. You can also often get a close to actual

Sample Budget Page

199 5

RENTS

Main Building	**ABC Properties**	
($16,198/mo. increases 3% on 8/1/95)		$ 196,806
Parking	**Parking Lots Inc.**	
(12 spaces at $40/mo.)		$ 480
Warehouse	**SuperStorage**	
($200/mo.)		$ 2,400
Equipment Rentals		
Postage meter rental **Pitney/Bowes**		$ 835
($412.50 twice a year, due 1/1 and 7/1)		
Copy machines **Xerox**		$ 4,272
($356/mo. expires 4/4/96)		
Telephone **Bell Communications**		$ 14,628
($1,219/mo. expires 7/1/97)		

TOTAL:	**$219,421**
Budget last year:	**$195,008**
Actual last year:	**$201,962**

number if the item is based on a contractual agreement and doesn't often vary. Be sure to consider automatic price increase clauses and other hidden costs often overlooked.

Wherever possible in our budget, we've listed the important financial points of the lease to make this process easier next year, and to let the accounting department know if these payments are expected to increase, stop or decrease at any point during the year.

Questions to ask

Have all important expense items been captured in the worksheet?

Are your preliminary estimates significantly over or under the actual numbers for last year?

Are explanatory notes understandable to anyone?

Are there any items that you find you are no longer using?

Are there any numbers that seem out of proportion to the value of the service you are paying for?

Look at total amounts paid to various vendors during your last full year. Will this year be about the same as last? Is there an automatic increase to any of these expenses?

Do you plan to use less of a given product or service next year?

Do you always pay a specific amount for a given product or service each month, or does it vary by the quantity used?

Are there new vendors you're negotiating with now that you plan to begin using in the near future? How will they compare with existing expense items?

INSURANCE POLICY AND PAYMENTS SCHEDULES

Overview

The goal of these two worksheets is to have all of the information pertaining to insurance policies summarized on one page and to have the payments listed by month on a second page.

The insurance worksheets will help you categorize insurance by type (also essential for categorizing your costs). They'll also help you remember when your policies need to renew and, considering your other expenditures, help you decide when it is convenient for you to pay for your insurance premiums over time.

Insurance costs — and, therefore, savings — can be great. The cost of insurance will go up and down depending on sales, total assets, total payroll, etc. Accurate budgeting may work to keep premium dollars under control.

Initially, you might choose to have your insurance agent or broker complete the worksheets for you.

Directions

I find it essential for planning another one of the larger expenditures faced by every business, to have all of the information pertaining to my insurance policies summarized in one location.

The first worksheet — the Insurance Policy Schedule — lists the major types of insurances most businesses choose (or are required) to carry on the left. The blank spaces are for you to fill in the types of policies you have that might be specific to your industry (for instance, we carry a publishers' liability policy).

Next, list the carrier (insurance company), the policy number, the expiration date (or in the case of life insurance, when the policy started), the total annual premium, policy limits, and deductibles, and an explanation of when the policies must be paid.

Insurance Policy Schedule

Type	Carrier	Limits	Deductible	Policy #	Expiration (or policy inception)	Yearly Premium
Insurance - L & H						
Medical						
Dental						
Disability						
Life						
Travel Accident						
					TOTAL . . .	
Insurance - P & C						
Commercial Package (property - liability)						
Commercial Auto						
Commercial Umbrella						
Employee Dishonesty Bond						
					TOTAL . . .	
Ins. - Workers Comp						
Workers Comp.						
Ins. - Officer's Life						
					TOTAL . . .	
					GRAND TOTAL . . .	

Taking Control Series Form # 17
1994 © The Merritt Company

Insurance Payments Schedule

Type	Carrier	Jan.	Feb.	Mar.	April	May	June	July	Aug.	Sept.	Oct.	Nov.	Dec.	Total
Total By Month:														

Keeping copies of this worksheet from year to year will allow you to see how much your insurance costs are increasing. Show these to your agent or broker, and ask for explanations.

Taking information from the Insurance Policy Schedule, the second worksheet — the Insurance Payments Schedule — will help you know when payments for each insurance policy come due. This will help you in planning your cash requirements.

It is important to note that any significant item of your expenses could be planned out like your insurance payments on this same type of worksheet.

Questions to ask

Could you carry higher deductibles to reduce premiums?

Are your limits of liability adequate to cover all of your assets?

Do you have all of the types of insurance your business requires?

Are there ways to reduce premiums by shopping for new carriers?

How will changes in payroll change your workers comp. insurance classifications and premiums?

PAYROLL PROJECTIONS

There is one piece of most budgets to which not everyone has access — that is the payroll. This makes it difficult to study for cost reduction as openly as you might any other budget item.

This worksheet will accurately project and document payroll, the largest area of expense for most companies.

It is important to project payroll accurately, not only because it is a significant expense in and of itself, but also because of its direct impact on many other expense categories. Payroll taxes, workers' comp insurance, life and disability insurance, and retirement plan expenses generally all fluctuate with changes in payroll.

To calculate payroll, ask each manager to determine the department's head count and payroll costs on the next worksheet. The worksheet gives columns for each employee's current salary (times a number of months) plus a column for a salary increase (times the number of months the higher salary will be in effect).

Adding the numbers in the last column gives you the total compensation of each department's employees for the year. Add below the actual payroll for that department last year.

Totaling the shaded box at the bottom right of each department worksheet will give you the total company payroll.

Payroll is rarely, if ever, reduced, except in crises. Employees never expect their salaries to be static. They generally expect their compensation to increase — at least once a year. These increases rarely respond to real productivity increases. They're part of an entitlement employees feel about their jobs, which most assume include a higher salary and greater benefits with each passing year.

Payroll Projections

Please use pencil.
Round figures to the nearest dollar.

Department _____

Employee Number	Employee Name	Current Monthly Salary (if hourly wage, convert to monthly*)	x # of mos.	= total at current salary	Next salary Increase (date)	x % inc.	Future Salary (if hourly wage, convert to monthly*)	x # of mos.	= total at new salary	TOTAL COMPENSATION (total shaded columns)

Total For Department [ ]

Actual for Department Last Year [ ]

• *Formula to convert hourly rate to monthly rate is: hourly rate x 173.3 (example $10.00 hr. x 173.3 = $1733. mo.)*

Taking Control Series Form # 19
1994 © The Merritt Company

Because of the always-growing nature of payrolls, many companies are experimenting with progressive compensation plans like performance-based pay. But, regardless of how you determine what you pay your employees, payroll must be projected to get an accurate profit picture.

Questions to ask

Are some departments' payrolls increasing more quickly than others? Is this due to additions to staff or pay increases? Is this in line with your overall growth plans?

Are your payroll dollars going to the areas you wish to emphasize?

Are managers realistic about the increases they want to give?

How much has your total payroll increased this year? In dollars? As a percentage? How will this affect other expenses?

PAYROLL BY CLASSIFICATION BY MONTH

This worksheet combines information provided by each manager and divides it by classifications relevant to how you want to look at your actual payroll expenses.

By breaking these sections of total payroll out separately, you can get clearer measurements of how much it costs to make your product, how much it costs to sell it, and what some of your administrative (overhead) costs are.

In addition, you should want to look at how payroll is spread out over time. Most entrepreneurs know exactly which weeks they need to cover their payroll. It's hard for most employees to understand, but if your payroll is $1 million a year (and a company of 35 people can easily have that), every two weeks the company sends out about $40,000 worth of paychecks.

My company pays employees every other Friday, which comes out to 26 paychecks a year. This generally means that employees get three paychecks in June and December, and two in every other month. Accordingly, our payroll on a cash basis is higher in June and December than in every other month. This becomes important to know if June is your lowest sales month.

Use your Payroll Projections worksheets by department to fill out this worksheet, employee by employee. Be careful to put their pay increases into the right months. Classify each employee in one of four ways:

- *Cost of Goods Sold* (salaries & wages) — the payroll of those employees who contribute directly to the production of the product

Payroll By Classification By Month

Cost of Goods Sold (salaries & wages)

Employee	Monthly Salary	Jan.	Feb.	Mar.	April	May	June	July	Aug.	Sept.	Oct.	Nov.	Dec.	Totals
Totals														

Sales & Marketing Expense (salaries)

Employee	Monthly Salary	Jan.	Feb.	Mar.	April	May	June	July	Aug.	Sept.	Oct.	Nov.	Dec.	Totals
Totals														

Overhead Expense (salaries)

Employee	Monthly Salary	Jan.	Feb.	Mar.	April	May	June	July	Aug.	Sept.	Oct.	Nov.	Dec.	Totals
Totals														

Officers' Salaries

Employee	Monthly Salary	Jan.	Feb.	Mar.	April	May	June	July	Aug.	Sept.	Oct.	Nov.	Dec.	Totals
Totals														

Grand Totals	Jan.	Feb.	Mar.	April	May	June	July	Aug.	Sept.	Oct.	Nov.	Dec.	

Taking Control Series Form # 20
1994 © The Merritt Company

- *Sales and Marketing Expense* (salaries) — salaries and commissions of sales and marketing employees

- *Overhead Expense* (salaries) — all other employees, not otherwise categorized

- *Officers' Salaries* — the owners and officers of the company should be categorized separately

Sum up the columns for the grand totals at the bottom of the page.

Do some months require significantly more dollars to meet payroll than others?

Is it possible to stagger pay increases throughout the year?

Are salary dollars spent making and selling the products, or is a lot more spent on administrative overhead?

In which months are incentive bonuses and other special compensation paid? How are different departments affected by these items?

Is your projected head-count higher or lower than last year? How will that influence other expenses?

Questions to ask

Total Company Projections

This exercise pulls together on one page all the items gathered in the budget notebook and looks overall at your profit picture.

Overview

Categorizing your expenses this way is important to begin to look at your overall profit picture as a number you can control.

From the information gathered in the budget notebook, you can begin to analyze your profit picture by putting your numbers in five major categories as follows:

Directions

- Sales
- Cost of goods sold
- Sales and marketing expenses
- Overhead expenses (including administration, personnel, facilities, etc.)
- Income before taxes
- Net income.

Cost of goods sold include the direct costs that go into producing your product. The percentage in the box next to this category is the complement of your gross profit margin. In other words, if your cost of good sold percentage is 69 percent, then your gross profit margin is 31 percent.

Sales and marketing expenses include what it costs you to market and sell your product. In some cases it costs more than the price of the product to sell it, and only in repeat business is there a reasonable profit margin. It is important to know so that you can price accordingly.

Overhead expenses include all other items such as personnel not in other categories, facilities costs, and administrative items such as office supplies, etc.

The *net income* at the bottom of the page should be a budget item, just like the rest of your expenses. I'm

Total Company Projections

Notebook Item	Current Year Projection	% of sales	Actual Last year	% of sales	Fixed (F) or Variable (V)?
Sales					
Cost of Goods Sold					
Beginning inventory					
Materials purchased					
Salaries & wages					
Production supplies					
Temporary help					
Shipping supplies					
Mailing & shipping					
Less ending inventory					
Total cost of goods sold					
Gross Profit					
Sales & Marketing Expenses					
Salaries					
Sales commissions					
Direct mail					
Advertising					
Publicity					
Consulting					
Other sales & marketing expense					
Total sales & marketing expense					
Overhead Expenses					
Personnel					
Salaries					
Bonuses					
Payroll taxes					
Group life & health insurance					
Workers comp. insurance					
Employee benefit plans					
Officers' salaries					
Employment expense					
Training					
Temporary help					
Total personnel					
Facilities					
Rents					
Property tax					
Repairs & maintenance					
Utilities					
Property & liability insurance					
Total facilities					
Administration					
Accounting services					
Automobiles					
Bank charges					
Computer supplies					
Contributions					
Depreciation & amortization					
Dues & subscriptions					
Legal services					
Licenses					
Miscellaneous					
Office supplies					
Other professional services					
Retirement plans					
Telephone					
Travel					
Total administration					
Total Overhead Expenses					
Income (Before Taxes)					
Income Taxes					
Net Income					

not satisfied unless this number is at least 15 percent, but this will vary by your industry, and the economy in general.

To obtain the current year projection (the shaded column), enter the total number from each budget notebook page you filled out for each category. For sales, enter the projection for this year and the actual for last year from the Dollar Sales Projections by Month worksheet (shaded box on bottom right for both years). For other categories, enter the projection number from each budget notebook page and the actual numbers from last year that you added to each budget notebook page.

Calculate the percentage of your total sales that each category makes up by dividing the total number at the bottom of each box by the total sales box at the top. You should have percentages for each of the items listed above, except sales.

The last column requires that you determine whether your costs are fixed or variable. Variable costs are those costs that are directly impacted by sales. These costs are expected to change, more or less, in proportion to the change in sales. An example: sales commissions. Fixed costs are all those that are not variable. They don't change as the level of sales increases or decreases. An example: Rent.

Some costs may have both a variable piece and a fixed piece. For example, utilities, which go up as equipment is used more to meet production demands but are relatively fixed for most of the office. For purposes of this analysis, expenses which could be either should be classified as fixed.

Are you satisfied with the dollar number and the percentage at the bottom of the page?

Are these numbers higher or lower than last year?

Compare these percentages with industry norms (see resources section in the appendix for sources). Are you higher or lower than others in your industry?

Are category totals as a percentage of sales higher or lower than you would expect?

Questions to ask

BREAKEVEN ANALYSIS

This worksheet determines the sales level at which the company neither makes a profit or suffers a loss.

Breakeven analysis can help to identify problems and avoid or lessen losses by acting proactively rather than reactively. Obviously, the sooner you recognize that the company is operating at less than breakeven operations, the sooner you can begin to cut fixed costs and take other measures to restore profitability.

Some companies use breakeven analysis in order to evaluate their overall profit goal. It is a simple-to-use tool to relate sales to profit. Breakeven analysis is driven by the relationship of costs, volumes, and profits.

Breakeven analysis offers a consistent way to test proposed transactions, consider alternatives or make decisions. Most of the information required to determine your breakeven already exists in your annual budget.

Use the previous Total Company Projections worksheet to determine which costs are fixed and which are variable.

On page one, you will determine the variable cost percentage. This can be done in two ways:

1) Divide the total variable costs by projected sales

   variable cost/sales = *variable cost percentage*

2) Using historical financial statements, divide all variable costs by sales to derive each variable cost as a percentage of sales. Then add all of these percentages to obtain a total variable cost percentage.

Breakeven Analysis — Page 1

% of sales (1)

Variable Expenses —
Materials purchased
Production supplies
Shipping supplies
Mailing & shipping
Sales commissions
Total variable cost %   %

Contribution Margin Ratio   %
(100% — total variable cost %)

Fixed Costs —
Monthly $
Annual $

Breakeven Sales Level —
(Fixed cost + contribution margin ratio)
Monthly $
Annual $

(1) Current year projections worksheet, % sales column, variable expenses only

Taking Control Series Form # 22
1994 © The Merritt Company

Breakeven Analysis — Page 2

	Annual	Monthly
Fixed Expenses $		
Personnel		
Salaries & wages — cost of sales		
Salaries — administration		
Bonuses		
Payroll taxes		
Group life & health insurance		
Workers comp. insurance		
Officers' salaries		
Employment expense		
Training		
Temporary labor		
Total personnel costs $		
Sales & Marketing Expenses		
Salaries		
Direct mail		
Advertising		
Publicity		
Consulting		
Other sales & marketing expense		
Total sales & marketing expense $		
Facilities Expenses		
Rents		
Property tax		
Repairs & maintenance		
Utilities		
Property & liability insurance		
Total facilities expenses $		
Administration		
Accounting services		
Automobiles		
Bank charges		
Computer supplies		
Contributions		
Depreciation & amortization		
Dues & subscriptions		
Interest expense		
Legal services		
Licenses		
Miscellaneous		
Office supplies		
Other professional services		
Retirement plans		
Telephone		
Travel		
Total administration expense $		
Total Fixed Expenses $		

(1) Current year projections column of *Total Company Projections* worksheet
(2) Current year projections divided by 12

Example:

Materials:	50 percent
Production:	10 percent
Direct Labor:	10 percent
Sales salaries:	5 percent

Total Variable Cost: 75 percent

The next step (on page two) is to determine the contribution margin ratio. This ratio is calculated by taking the complement of the variable cost percentage, or simply, subtracting the variable cost percentage from 100 percent.

Contribution Margin Ratio = 100 percent minus the variable cost percent

Now you are ready to calculate your sales breakeven level. To do this, divide total fixed costs by the contribution margin ratio.

Sales Breakeven Level = total fixed costs/ contribution margin ratio

Questions to ask

If sales begin to decline, at what level will you start to lose money?

If you increase fixed costs by $X, how much additional sales will you need to generate to cover these costs?

If you lower the variable cost percentage, what impact will it have on profits?

If you want a profit of $X, what level of sales will you have to achieve?

CHAPTER 4: FINANCIAL SCOREKEEPING

The goal of every business, stated simply, is to make money. The extent to which your business does this will determine your success — and your ability to stay in business. Making money can be defined in two ways: making a profit and generating cash. Profitable businesses usually generate cash, but not always. Unprofitable businesses sometimes generate cash, but not often.

Either way, in reviewing your finances, you look at both profits and cash. This chapter takes you through this review by stressing three points:

- The importance of setting budgets and tracking variances from budgeted amounts;

- The importance of cash in running any business; and

- The central role of developing financial indicators and communicating them to coworkers.

Choosing your financial indicators depends on the kind of business you run and whether your company is young or mature. As a rule, cash is king for a young company; many startup owners fear running out of cash more than anything else. In a mature company, sales and growth may become the main concern. When a company goes public, showing a good return on assets may become paramount.

Flying Blind

The owners of many new businesses fly blind, concentrating on the day to day essentials at the expense of planning. But once they do start to plan, they discover that the process brings unexpected payoffs in reaching their goals — because planning forces them to identify what they want and discover the means by which to get there.

Tracking profits and cash

A long term blueprint

Effective managers develop their own methods for gauging performance, and they define performance in accordance with their short and long term goals. They may consider daily revenues, for example, or catalogs mailed, cash balance, and payroll.

If you run a startup, you can use your financials to track cash; if a mature company, to track growth. Whatever the measure, the small business owner must become intimately involved in daily dynamics of the business. This familiarity provides a long term blueprint for keeping the company vital, because the god — or maybe the devil — of implementation is in the details.

Every review must cover accounts payable (people to whom you owe money), accounts receivable (people who owe money to you), and cash availability. Inherent in any such review is the ability to track change, since it is change that gives meaning to the numbers.

Make sure you get your financials done monthly, and preferably by the fifteenth of the following month, at the latest. Learn which pieces of information in them are relevant to your business and concentrate on those. Don't ignore what the numbers tell you, and above all, believe them; good or bad, the numbers are important. Don't hesitate to shape the reports you get to suit your ends, either. Accountants tend to work by habit, and they sometimes prepare numbers for business managers without giving much thought to making them truly useful.

The Basics

The traditional financial statement has two components — the income statement and the balance sheet. The income statement shows your sales and expenses for a given period, usually the month, the quarter or the year. The balance sheet shows net worth; it also details such items as inventory, fixed assets, accounts payable, and accounts receivable.

In both cases, your financials look backward to show the present — namely your position as of their date of preparation.

To complete the exercises and worksheets in this section, you'll need:

- Your income statement and balance sheet;
- A list of your accounts payable; and
- A list of your accounts receivable.

You may need to gather other data as well. The worksheets and formulas which flow from this information will help you:

- Compare projections to actual sales and expenses through your fiscal year;
- Analyze cash flow;
- Calculate and analyze various financial ratios; and
- Determine key financial indicators and other information critical to managers and employees.

Put together, the worksheets and exercises provide you with useful financial tools which will allow you to monitor your company's performance from many different perspectives.

Concentrating the Mind

There's nothing like a brush with disaster to show you what matters and what doesn't, as the Wisconsin-based Carson Pirie Scott department store chain learned during a bankruptcy reorganization in 1991. The exercise taught management to improve performance by paying close attention to the company's real-time financial position — key in retailing with its turnover and stiff competition.

Michael MacDonald, chief financial officer, tracks sales and cash position on a monthly, even a weekly basis.

"You really have to manage a business on a detailed basis and on a frequent basis," MacDonald says. "You don't just look at it now and again. You have to look at it all the time — every day."

The company used a five-inch-thick business plan to chart its way out of bankruptcy. Its creditors in-

'Retail is detail'

sisted that the retailer remain wary of variances from budget. The business plan, MacDonald says, became the company's road map away from disaster.

"There's an axiom in retail that says retail is detail," MacDonald says. "You need to track sales on hand on a very detailed basis. We have pretty sophisticated methods to check what sizes and colors are selling."

For key indicators, managers chart sales per square foot, comparable-store sales growth (to show market share), and operating profit as a percentage of sales and earnings.

Cash and inventory "require continuous fine tuning and monitoring," MacDonald says. The challenge is to make sure that the shortage of cash doesn't choke off the flow of in-demand products.

He describes the goal of his financial scorekeeping bluntly: "The main purpose of a business is to maximize shareholder or investor value." But he watches a number of indicators to achieve that end, all tied to what the company calls the three keys to successful retailing—effective merchandising, giving the customer a positive shopping experience, and marketing.

A Positive Experience

Good merchandising means offering the right product at the right price. Competition in retailing keeps pricing pretty rigid, MacDonald says, so there's not much room for maneuvering here. Giving the customer a positive shopping experience means making the stores pleasant and allowing the customer to get in and out quickly. To Carson Pirie Scott, marketing means getting the customer to come back again and again. MacDonald does much of his scorekeeping here.

"We've put in place what we call loyalty programs, designed to get customers to continue to shop with us, " he says. "It's very costly to acquire new customers and a lot cheaper to get more sales dollars out of existing customers. We've spent about $14 million over the last 18 months on our point of sale system to make it simple to operate. That makes it simpler and easier for our associates, which helps us reduce training time. And it also quickens the transaction time at the point of sale."

MacDonald watches transaction time closely. He also monitors the mix of promotional discounts the company uses to keep product flowing through the stores.

"We're a highly promotional department store and we will always be that way. But we have tightened up our promotions so they are of shorter duration and have more impact and demonstrate a sense of urgency to the customer," he says. "We discount hot selling items at their peak selling time, whereas before we might have tried to milk it at full price. We take a singular hot item and mark it down for a very short term event as a way of giving extra value to the customer."

The attention to detail paid off. In 1993, Carson Pirie Scott had earnings of about $33 million on sales of $1.15 billion — not stellar numbers, but on target with management's goals to avert disaster.

Key Indicators

One key to the success of the Carson Pirie Scott effort was its ability to limit an important shortcoming in financial analysis—the fact that the numbers lag actual performance. Carson Pirie Scott knew that if it tracked expenses, for example, only at the end of each quarter, it would do so too late to make a difference; if you don't look at the money you spend until after you spend it, you look too late.

The financials also can't answer qualitative questions such as those that go into the formulation of your company's vision statement. And you may well find that your financial statement and balance sheet don't address other matters of concern to you. If so, you may need to analyze such items as your return on invested capital, or quality, market share, and customer satisfaction.

Among the indicators owners and managers find most key:

Budgets set cost targets

Net Income. Always a key indicator of financial performance, it reflects sales and costs, profit and loss — the best places to start any analysis.

Cash position. Especially in the early years of a company's history, liquidity has more importance than any other financial benchmark. But whatever the maturity of your company, it pays to watch how much money you have in the bank at least monthly and maybe weekly.

Accounts payable and accounts receivable. Many experts call these leading indicators since they give you a read on what your cash position will be next month. However, accounts receivable are sometimes collected more slowly than payables come due — in which case your cash position becomes tight.

Net worth. This indicator — which, in publicly-traded companies is called shareholders' equity — is simply assets minus liabilities. It includes equity put into the business through the sale of stock or retained earnings. It helps you consider the best ways to allocate equity and assets in order to reach your goals.

Implicit in this discussion is the fact that your concentration on the financials may blind you to opportunity. Budgets set cost targets, leading some managers to spend their time controlling how much the operation spends and ignoring how much it earns — or might. They monitor money going out and forget about the profit and loss statement, which shows results. Worse, they ignore the balance sheet, which shows your financial position.

If this becomes single-mindedness, it has long-term costs. It turns an organization inward, values rules above initiative and leads managers to query trivial variances while they ignore harder-to-identify, company-wide problems or opportunities. Financial measurements must always be balanced against measures of operations, product development and marketing.

The Essentials

Robert Espenschield, CEO of Business Essentials, Inc., a small Missouri-based office supply retailer, knows the value of watching cash flow in a new venture. After working for eight years at a larger supply company, he decided he could carve out a niche for himself by offering select customers low prices and a high level of service.

In 1993, Business Essentials had revenues of over $1 million. Espenschield predicted annual sales of over $2 million for 1994 — significantly ahead of his original projections. He attributes his success most of all to a close watch of cash flow. "A cash flow statement and financial statement — you really can't determine if a business is going to make it without those pieces of information," he says.

The company's mission statement:

> *To sell office supplies to customers for a lower price and provide them a better service. We sell at lower margins than our competition yet make more money. Anything from pencils and paper to tables and chairs.*

"I investigated with potential vendors and when I looked at their profit margins I knew I could compete because I knew what customers were willing to pay," Espenschield says.

He and his partner wrote their business plan on a computer and showed it to the Small Business Administration. "We thought they were going to tear it apart," he says. "But one of the SBA consultants read it and thought it looked good. He told us it should have a cash flow statement since it didn't at the time."

Low Overhead

It was good advice. The SBA sent the partners to a bank for $100,000 in startup money, most of it to cover salaries for one year. One of the company's strengths is its ability to keep overhead low. "We don't have a large corporate office we are subsidizing," Espenschield says. "And since we've been able

Check for variances

to limit our supply to very few items, we're still able to supply service better than anyone else."

He relies on bottom-line profit margin to make certain decisions such as when to hire new staff. The company tries to keep accounts receivable at a tight 30 days. Customers pay one sum per month, not per order.

The company employs six people in 2,000 square feet of office space. It stocks certain high-dollar products that it can turn over quickly.

"We actually have exceeded benchmarks of our plan so we've had to revise it," Espenschield says. "We showed in the business plan how we planned to compete with the large contract stationers such as the one we came from.

"We had our business plan a year and a half, and we just updated it. We should probably update it every year. Our initial plan was only for three years," he says. The next one will probably be for five."

The company's biggest financial concern is the bank loan its founders took to get things started.

"We'll probably be free and clear within a couple years, mainly because we're reinvesting most of the profits in our business," Espenschield says. "It's a five year loan, but we'll probably pay it off two years in advance. We got it pretty cheap, about 7.5 percent. First it was at 8, then we refinanced. We told the banker to do it or we would take our business to another."

Monitoring Expenses

The purpose of making projections is to use them continually to monitor and adjust performance. This means looking at sales and expense numbers along with your monthly financial statement, and checking for variances between the forecast and actual performance, so that you can adjust accordingly.

Many small business owners don't think critically when they run into cash flow problems. Instead, they react by trying to boost sales. They chase revenue, and cost be damned. In so doing they overextend themselves seeking new business and fail to serve their best customers. This can harm cash flow — the last thing a company needs if liquidity's already a problem.

There are other ways to maximize cash flow, chief among them controlling expenses. Many business owners see expense controls as a sign of trouble, but they aren't. The *absence* of cost controls is a sign of trouble.

"If you don't have cash flow, you can actually grow out of business," says Ball State University professor Donald Kuratko. "If money isn't being collected, it can cause a cash crunch. Even though sales might be up and customers are happy with your product, none of that matters if all your profits are on credit."

If you find your business short of cash, look to your balance sheet and study receivables and inventory — common drains on cash flow. Without adequate controls over inventory, you can make a profit and still go out of business. Whenever possible, integrate your inventory management with customer service and delivery programs. The object: Keep only those units on your warehouse shelves that you expect to sell in the short term. Manufacturers sometimes lose a significant part of the value of their inventory covering the costs of loans and borrowed money. Borrowing costs don't always stand out in ordinary financial statements, so some companies don't discover the problem until they've already absorbed the costs.

Sound Borrowing

Review your borrowing strategy as well, because this, too, influences cash flow. Sound borrowing means projecting your requirements and using your cash forecasts to assure repayment. How much you borrow, when and under what terms — all figure into your cash and profit positions. Remember the old rule of thumb: Don't finance long-term assets with short-term borrowing.

Good practice pays dividends

Years ago, businesses went to banks when they needed financing. And banks lent to businesses about which they didn't know much, securing their loans with such assets as residential real estate. Now cash is king in bank lending.

"Banks used to look at a business loan on the basis of the borrower's net worth," says a corporate banking officer at one of Colorado's biggest banks. "Today, they're looking at cash flow: the ability to service debt and pay interest. Ten years ago, they'd take real estate or anything as collateral. Today, the collateral isn't as important as the cash flow and the ability [to repay]."

To qualify for an unsecured line of credit for working capital, you must identify the purpose of the loan and show your lender financial statements illustrating cash flow sufficient to service it. For expansion capital, you must show a business plan projecting a sufficient return on the investment. With loans for working or expansion capital, your company's numbers are crucial. Your lender must see that you can generate cash to repay the loan. (For equity capital from private sources, your business plan must show your own investment, among other things.)

Accounts Receivable and Payable

Your management of receivables and payables profoundly affects your cash flow. Poor management here can kill almost any company, no matter what the size, and good management pays big dividends. Just by managing receivables well, even in a small company, you can generate tremendous amounts of cash—in today's economy, the name of the game.

With receivables, a few basic rules apply:

- Develop a good credit-checking system.
- Send your bills out faster, and follow up with phone calls when an account becomes overdue.
- Establish a strict collections schedule and follow it faithfully.
- Keep managers and employees informed when collections become difficult with products they develop, make or sell. They may help with strategies for collecting.

In the case of accounts payable, most small companies manage efficiently by necessity. They pay as much of their bills as often as they can — in dire circumstances, the only way to go. If you make so much money that you simply pay your bills without thinking, you should take a step back.

Standard practice is to pay bills within thirty days of receipt (or earlier, if the vendor offers a discount for early payment). If you take more time than this, some vendors charge financing fees. Some stop supplying you with the things you need to stay in business.

Many frugal companies pay between thirty and forty-five days after receipt — if they're careful about which vendors they delay for how long.

Perhaps the best use of accounts receivable and payable as a management tool is to compare the two. Average the time it takes you to pay your bills and the time it takes you to collect. If it takes longer to collect accounts receivable than pay your bills, you're subsidizing customers. If it takes you longer to pay than collect, you're effectively making money from the process.

But be careful about managing cash flow by manipulating receivables and payables. There's a long term cost to not paying your bills on time. Especially in tight industry niches, word travels about who pays on time and who doesn't. The day may come when you need a favor from a vendor who feels ill used or when a credit agency down-grades your payment rating.

Inventory

Another way to look at the receivables/payables ratio is as a measure of your financial department's efficiency. Your accounting people must make sure the company pays its bills and collects its receivables on time.

Another cash drain is excess inventory. Without adequate controls over receivables and inventory, it's entirely possible for a company to make a profit and still go out of business.

Tracking cash flow every day

Whenever and as much as possible, you should integrate inventory management with customer service and delivery programs. The object: To keep as few units on warehouse shelves as you can.

The cost of carrying inventory is expensive. Some manufacturing companies pay 25 to 30 percent of the value of their inventory for the cost of borrowed money, warehouse space, materials handling, staff and transportation expenses related to maintaining it for one financial quarter — three months.

These numbers shock people. Once they realize how expensive inventory can be, they look at it differently. But many owners and managers never make this realization because the cost doesn't show up on any statement. They have to calculate it themselves.

Scrupulous Monitoring

Unity Forest Products, Inc., a California-based lumber company, thrives by scrupulously monitoring its cash flow and related items such as inventory, accounts receivable and accounts payable. In a volatile business, it combines efficiency, knowledge of its customers' needs and close attention to financial detail to succeed. Despite that volatility and the plight of the lumber industry in general, the company has never had an unprofitable month.

The company makes sure that profit centers stay profitable. Its employees work hard, producing some 6 million board feet of lumber each month. CEO Enita Nordeck tracks cash flow each day herself.

Unity started out as a bootstrap operation run by a collection of longtime mill workers who didn't fear competing with the industry's big players. Lumber is a heavily-capitalized, low margin business, and bootstrappers don't usually have the money to get in the game.

Nordeck and her crew needed $1 million to get started. In 1987, when starting out, the management team had only $350,000 in cash. For a short time, Unity bought lumber from sawmills, subcontracted out the resawing, then sold the wood wholesale to lumberyards.

Nordeck had refined a just-in-time inventory management concept into a five-year business plan which depended on weekly cash flow projections — unusual for any startup, let alone one in a volatile commodity business. Unity claimed it could turn inventory over every ten days; the industry average was 58. The company also claimed it could collect accounts receivable in ten days; the industry average was 27.

Management looked everywhere for cash to build a new mill but had trouble persuading lenders to back its plan, which lenders considered so aggressive that they doubted its projections. Wells Fargo approved a $150,000 credit line which Unity never touched. Finally the bank lent Unity the cash to get started.

Nordeck offers her customers a 1 percent discount if they pay within 10 days. In turn, it gets a 2 percent discount from suppliers if Unity pays within ten days. Competitors see that Unity has figured out that the most significant expense in the lumber industry is carrying a lot of inventory.

Unity also keeps close track of receivables. At one point, a customer who owed the company $40,000 was about to declare bankruptcy. Unity managers drove several company trucks to the customer's plant and repossessed the lumber before sheriff's deputies could arrive to lock up the facility.

The Bottom Line

Many owners and managers are experts at product costs but not with everyday, nonspecific business costs. You can hire consultants or professional staff to study your costs of labor, capital and the rest, but you still need a basic approach to these issues. And you have to know how to judge the results of their work.

Financial matters sometimes conflict with your vision and mission statements. When this happens, you may have to acknowledge the limits of quantitative analysis. Look to your business plan and vision

Value/ cost analysis

and mission statements for guidance in making value-driven cost analysis.

Simply said, value/cost analysis is an approach to valuing items which defy deductive assessment.

YEAR AT A GLANCE INCOME STATEMENT

The income statement tells you how well your company has done over a period of time. It shows both your revenue and your expenses, and arrives at a net income number at the bottom of the page.

Financial reports done by your accountants are useful comparing this year to last year, but they don't tell you whether there is a big variation from projection and which month the variation may have occurred. If there is a large variation in one month, the year to date numbers are off the rest of the year after that point.

The worksheet synthesizes a number of important numbers into one form — on one page. It offers a visual way to look at everything at once, which helps you think about business activities over the course of a whole year. Large variances become quickly apparent.

Using this worksheet, I find myself better prepared to ask pointed questions about budget items. I can compare them to other items, even other budget variances.

Of course, some of these items may result from miscoding and similar technical problems, rather than expenses being much different than expected. But even glitches become easier to detect when the numbers run alongside one another.

Enter your actual sales and expense numbers each month throughout the year. Calculate the monthly average column by taking the number of months into the year you are, and dividing by that number.

This tells you if your monthly average is over your original budget, and whether your current month is above or below average.

Year At A Glance Income Statement — Page 1

	Jan.	Feb.	March	April	May	June	July	Aug.	Sept.	Oct.	Nov.	Dec.	Total	Mo. Avg.
Sales														
Cost of Goods Sold														
Beginning inventory														
Materials purchased														
Salaries & wages														
Production supplies														
Temporary help														
Shipping supplies														
Mailing & shipping														
Less ending inventory														
Total cost of goods sold														
Gross Profit														
Sales & Marketing Expenses														
Salaries														
Sales commissions														
Direct mail														
Advertising														
Publicity														
Consulting														
Other sales & marketing expense														
Total sales & marketing expense														
Overhead Expenses														
Personnel														
Salaries														
Bonuses														
Payroll taxes														
Group life & health insurance														
Workers comp. insurance														
Employee benefit plans														
Officers' salaries														
Employment expense														
Training														
Temporary help														
Total personnel														

Year At A Glance Income Statement — Page 2

	Jan.	Feb.	March	April	May	June	July	Aug.	Sept.	Oct.	Nov.	Dec.	Total	Mo. Avg.
Facilities														
Rents														
Property tax														
Repairs & maintenance														
Utilities														
Property & liability insurance														
Total facilities														
Administration														
Accounting services														
Automobiles														
Bank charges														
Computer supplies														
Contributions														
Depreciation & amortization														
Dues & subscriptions														
Legal services														
Licenses														
Miscellaneous														
Office supplies														
Other professional services														
Retirement plans														
Telephone														
Travel														
Total administration														
Total Overhead Expenses														
Income (Before Taxes)														
Income Taxes														
Net Income														

Questions to ask

Are your expenses what you expected, or are there large variations?

Does each month look comparable, or are there large differences month to month?

Do particular items seem out of line with the others in the report?

Can you see trends that run across your business functions?

Are there certain budget items that play well compared against one another? What do those comparisons mean about your business functions?

Year at a Glance Balance Sheet

Overview

This worksheet illustrates items in your balance sheet in a format for easy analysis, month to month. It's a statement of what the company owns at a fixed point in time. It remains important to look at changes occurring from month to month because there is a direct relationship between changes in your balance sheet and your cash flow.

The Year at a Glance Balance Sheet allows you to track balance sheet accounts for trends. It also allows you a measurement system to track goals you may have to decrease inventory, or decrease accounts receivable (both of which would increase your cash).

Directions

The most important accounts to focus on are cash, accounts receivable, inventory, fixed assets and accounts payable. More obscure accounts like Other Assets generally don't change much month to month, so you don't need to focus on them. This format allows you to see important changes if they occur.

Most smaller and more aggressive owners and managers pay close attention to accounts receivable and payable on this worksheet. They affect cash flow in mercilessly direct ways:

- If accounts receivable go up — your cash goes down

- If inventory goes down — your cash goes up

- If accounts payable goes down — your cash goes down

- If fixed assets go up — your cash goes down.

Find the items below from your monthly balance sheet and enter each month on the worksheet. You will usually find these items on the balance sheet di-

Year At A Glance Balance Sheet

	Jan.	Feb.	Mar.	April	May	June	July	Aug.	Sept.	Oct.	Nov.	Dec.
ASSETS												
Cash												
Accounts Receivable												
Inventory												
Prepaid Expenses												
Other Current Assets												
Total Current Assets												
Fixed Assets												
Accumulated Depreciation												
Net Fixed Assets												
Intangible Assets												
Other Assets												
TOTAL ASSETS												
LIABILITIES												
Current Portion Long-Term Debt												
Notes Payable												
Accounts Payable												
Accrued Liabilities												
Other Current Liabilities												
Total Current Liabilities												
Long Term Debt												
Other Liabilities												
Total Liabilities												
EQUITY												
Common Stock												
Paid in Capital												
Retained Earnings												
TOTAL EQUITY AND LIABILITIES												

Taking Control Series Form # 26
1994 © The Merritt Company

vided by current (usually one year or less) or long term.

ASSETS

Current Assets

   Cash

   Accounts Receivable — money owed to you by your customers

   Inventory — your product waiting to be sold, either at your location or at a store

   Prepaid Expenses — items such as insurance or taxes (example: an insurance premium is paid up front for a whole year; this entry spreads it out over the policy period)

   Other Current Assets — miscellaneous items like rent deposits

Fixed Assets — real property, equipment and leasehold improvements

Accumulated Depreciation

Net Fixed Assets

Intangible Assets — good will, intellectual property — rights to something, trademarks, patents

LIABILITIES

Current Liabilities — an amount you owe to someone else, generally to be paid within 1 year

   Notes Payable

   Accounts Payable

   Accrued Liabilities

Long Term Debt

EQUITY

Retained Earnings — the amount of net income the company has earned and kept since the first day of the business, less dividends to shareholders

Questions to ask

Are your accounts receivable and accounts payable accounts up or down over the period?

Are there sharp variations during certain peak periods or seasons?

Is your cash consistently at a comfortable level for operating the business?

What is the current trend in inventory levels?

Has your company acquired fixed assets in accordance with capital budgets?

Year at a Glance Financial Analysis

This exercise pulls together useful information from both the balance sheet and income statement and calculates some ratios to give you an idea of the financial health of the company and how it changes month to month.

The ratios included here are generally computed for whole industries. It is useful to compare your numbers to your industry.

The Balance Sheet items are asset management related and tell you how well you are doing increasing the value of what you own. The Income Statement items are related to profitability and tell you how well you are doing in that area.

This worksheet, as with the other year at a glance worksheets, gives you a quick indication of how things are changing over time. The problem with financial statements is that you can't tell whether things have gotten better this month or worse. These will let you know immediately if there is a sudden downturn or a trend in that direction so that you can take corrective action.

Find the numbers for the first four categories from your income statement and enter them for the appropriate month. Also enter the number of people you currently employ. Divide sales by number of employees to get the number for the last category under the Income Statement, sales per employee.

Enter the numbers for the first three entries under Balance Sheet. The remainder of the categories are calculated as follows:

Sales. Take this item from your Income Statement.

Gross Profit Margin. This ratio is Sales minus Cost of Goods Sold divided by Sales.

Year At A Glance Financial Analysis

		Jan.	Feb.	Mar.	April	May	June	July	Aug.	Sept.	Oct.	Nov.	Dec.
	Income Statement												
1.	Sales												
2.	Gross Profit Margin												
3.	Pre Tax Profit												
4.	Cumulative Net Income												
5.	Number of Employees												
6.	Sales Per Employee												
	Balance Sheet												
7.	Total Current Assets												
8.	Total Current Liabilities												
9.	Working Capital												
10.	Current Ratio												
11.	Sales to Assets												
12.	Return on Assets												
13.	Debt to Equity												
14.	Accounts Receivable Days												
15.	Accounts Payable Days												
16.	Inventory Turnover (annually)												
17.	Inventory Turn Days												

Taking Control Series Form # 27
1994 © The Merritt Company

Pre-tax profit. Take this item from your Income Statement.

Cumulative Net Income. An aggregate of the monthly income figures listed for the year to date, this tells you how close you are to your projections for the year.

Number of Employees. Take this item from your Payroll Projection worksheets.

Sales per Employee. This number divides your sales figure by the number of people the company employs to generate that figure. This is a popular tool for determining a company's efficiency — though standards change dramatically by industry.

Total Current Assets. Take this item from your Balance Sheet.

Total Current Liabilities. Take this item from your Balance Sheet.

Working Capital. The amount by which Current Assets exceed Current Liabilities.

Current Ratio. A basic test of solvency, you obtain this number by dividing the current assets of your company by current liabilities.

Sales to Assets. A measure of how aggressively the business pursues sales, this figure (Total Current Assets divided by Sales) helps analysts determine how much unrealized sales potential a company might have.

Return on Assets. This figure (Pre Tax Profit divided by Total Assets) compares profit with the amount of assets used to earn that profit. Acceptable figures vary from industry to industry.

Debt to Equity. This figure (Total Liabilities divided by Net Worth or Shareholders' Equity) relates the company's debt to the strength of the equity in the company by owners or stockholders.

Accounts Receivable Days. First, divide Sales by Accounts Receivable to obtain accounts receivable turnover. Then, divide 365 by the turnover figure. The result (also called Collection Period Ratio) indicates how many days people are taking to pay you.

Accounts Payable Days. First, divide your Cost of Goods Sold by Accounts Payable to obtain accounts payable turnover. Then, divide 365 by the turnover figure. The result indicates how many days you're taking to pay your bills. It also tells analysts about your company's liquidity.

Inventory Turnover (annually). This figure (Cost of Goods Sold divided by the Inventory item from your Balance Sheet) provides an indicator of how many times a year your company turns over its entire inventory.

Inventory Turn Days. Obtained by dividing 365 by the annual Inventory Turnover figure, this figure gives you a time period to compare directly with the Accounts Receivable and Payable numbers listed above.

Clearly, this worksheet will be one of the most valuable when you're dealing with potential lenders or investors (also financial consultants who bill by the hour). In this context, financial analysts sometimes ask for ratios not included on this worksheet. Some of the most important include:

Current liabilities/inventory. Obtained by dividing current liabilities by the value of current inventory, this figure tells managers how much the company relies on funds yet to be obtained from unsold inventories to meet its debt obligations.

Net sales/working capital. By measuring the number of times working capital turns over annually in relation to net sales, this ratio provides information about whether the business relies too heavily on credit to maintain its sales effort.

Return on Investment. This figure prorates net profit by an individual investment vehicle's percentage of a company's total capitalization. It tells investors how soon they will recoup their money; it tells managers what form investments should take (limited partnerships, preferred or common stock, etc.).

Current liabilities/net worth. Considered by some lenders the most important test of a company's solvency, this figure indicates the amount due creditors within a year as a percentage of the investment in the business by owners or stockholders.

Questions to ask

Which numbers are trended in a positive direction, and which in a negative direction? Are your ratios in line with industry averages?

Which ratios concern you most? Are these issues which require immediate solutions (for example: the current ratio) or long-term solutions (for example: sales per employee)?

Is the overall financial condition of the company getting better or worse?

Can unusual or negative trends be explained satisfactorily?

Budget Variance Report

This worksheet gives an easy way to compare your actual numbers each month to your budget numbers, both for that month and the year to date (cumulative for the whole year).

Managers go through all the effort of making a budget each year, but unless they compare their actual financial picture to what they budgeted, doing the budget remains a meaningless exercise. Budget variance is a wake up call for managers to make mid-course corrections, and to replan for the remainder of the year. With any variance, a manager should investigate into what's gone right or wrong, and hold people accountable for their spending.

This worksheet is also very illustrative for employee meetings and board of directors meetings.

Overview

Enter your budget numbers for each item for the current month. Then enter the actual numbers that correspond to each category. In the third column, take the difference between the two (actual minus plan), and enter it in the "$ variance" column. For expense items, a negative number means you're under budget and a positive number means you spent more than you expected.

Lastly, calculate the "% variance" by dividing the "$ variance" by the "plan $." A negative "$ variance" will result in a negative "% variance." Complete the whole exercise again for year-to-date numbers.

Notice that all the reports in this section have the same categories in the same order as the original budget. This makes comparisons between budget and actual much easier.

Directions

Budget Variance Report — Page 1

	Month To Date				Year To Date			
	Plan $	Actual $	$ Variance	% Variance	Plan $	Actual $	$ Variance	% Variance

Sales

Cost of Goods Sold
- Beginning inventory
- Materials purchased
- Salaries & wages
- Production supplies
- Temporary help
- Shipping supplies
- Mailing & shipping
- Less ending inventory
- Total cost of goods sold

Gross Profit

Sales & Marketing Expenses
- Salaries
- Sales commissions
- Direct mail
- Advertising
- Publicity
- Consulting
- Other sales & marketing expense
- Total sales & marketing expense

Overhead Expenses

Personnel
- Salaries
- Bonuses
- Payroll taxes
- Group life & health insurance
- Workers comp. insurance
- Employee benefit plans
- Officers' salaries
- Employment expense
- Training
- Temporary help
- Total personnel

Facilities
- Rents
- Property tax
- Repairs & maintenance
- Utilities
- Property & liability insurance
- Total facilities

Taking Control Series Form # 28
1994 © The Merritt Company

Budget Variance Report — Page 2

	Month To Date				Year To Date			
	Plan $	Actual $	$ Variance	% Variance	Plan $	Actual $	$ Variance	% Variance
Administration								
Accounting services								
Automobiles								
Bank charges								
Computer supplies								
Contributions								
Depreciation & amortization								
Dues & subscriptions								
Legal services								
Licenses								
Miscellaneous								
Office supplies								
Other professional services								
Retirement plans								
Telephone								
Travel								
Total administration								
Total Overhead Expenses								
Income (Before Taxes)								
Income Taxes								
Net Income								

Questions to ask

Are there variances from budget of 10 percent or more (and $500 or more)? What accounts for these?

If these variances are in the Year To Date column, are they also in the current month, or did they take place in a prior month?

Are variances in Cost of Goods Sold influencing your gross profit margin?

Are your variances in the areas most companies find difficulty to control: sales, marketing and personnel?

Same Month Last Year Variance Report

Overview

This exercise allows comparison between individual months this year with the same months last year. This comparison allows for cyclical trends and historical perspective that many managers use as a basis for forecasting.

It's important to compare your current numbers to prior years, especially when you're trying to grow a company. At publicly-traded companies, stockholders always want to see if the company is doing better than last year.

Budgets can be wildly above or below actual performance. Unforeseen factors can change the business a company does in a given time period. Projections — even good ones — are always suspect. Last year's actuals are reality.

Directions

For the same month last year, enter your sales and expense numbers. Then use the same numbers from the Budget Variance worksheet to fill in the second column for the current month. Subtract last year from this year, and divide that number by last year to get the percent difference. A positive percentage indicates an increase from last year to this year.

Do the same calculations again with year-to-date numbers.

If the variance is great, again, do some investigation into what changed from last year.

Same Month Last Year Variance Report — Page 1

	Month To Date			Year To Date		
	Last Year $	This Year $	% Difference	Last Year $	This Year $	% Difference

Sales

Cost of Goods Sold

Beginning inventory

Materials purchased

Salaries & wages

Production supplies

Temporary help

Shipping supplies

Mailing & shipping

Less ending inventory

Total cost of goods sold

Gross Profit

Sales & Marketing Expenses

Salaries

Sales commissions

Direct mail

Advertising

Publicity

Consulting

Other sales & marketing expense

Total sales & marketing expense

Overhead Expenses

Personnel

Salaries

Bonuses

Payroll taxes

Group life & health insurance

Workers comp. insurance

Employee benefit plans

Officers' salaries

Employment expense

Training

Temporary help

Total personnel

Facilities

Rents

Property tax

Repairs & maintenance

Utilities

Property & liability insurance

Total facilities

Taking Control Series Form # 30
1994 © The Merritt Company

Same Month Last Year Variance Report — Page 2

	Month To Date			Year To Date		
	Last Year $	This Year $	% Difference	Last Year $	This Year $	% Difference
Administration						
Accounting services						
Automobiles						
Bank charges						
Computer supplies						
Contributions						
Depreciation & amortization						
Dues & subscriptions						
Legal services						
Licenses						
Miscellaneous						
Office supplies						
Other professional services						
Retirement plans						
Telephone						
Travel						
Total administration						
Total Overhead Expenses						
Income (Before Taxes)						
Income Taxes						
Net Income						

Questions to ask

Are there variances that are greater than 10 percent? If so, can you explain them in a way that makes sense?

Are your expenses up in any one category more than another?

If the variance comes in the Year To Date column, in what month did it begin to occur?

TOP 20 CUSTOMERS WHO OWE US MONEY

Overview

This worksheet keeps close track of the accounts receivable and helps to set a strategy to collect the money as soon as possible.

It is important to carefully track customers who bought your company's product on credit but haven't paid as they have agreed to within a specific time. The older the bills get, the less likely they will be paid.

It's important for managers to have a plan to get people to pay, and the first step in that is to know who owes money, how long they've owed it, and how much they owe. Sometimes the top 20 can account for most of the money owed to a company, if it has several large customers.

Doing something as simple as concentrating on getting paid by these people can have a significant impact on raising a company's cash position.

Directions

List the customers who owe you money and rank them from the largest dollar volume to the smallest. Enter the top ten, from largest to smallest on this worksheet.

Across the columns, show the total these customers owe and their balances (that equal this total) in each category of days overdue.

In the comments section, list their likelihood of paying, when you last contacted them, etc.

At the bottom of the worksheet, calculate how much money the top 20 represent compared to your total receivables.

169

Date _____

Top 20 Customers Who Owe Us Money
(Accounts Receivable Ranked by $ Volume)

Name	Customer Account #	Total Dollar Amount Owed	Past Due Balances				Comments
			30	60	90	120+	
1.							
2.							
3.							
4.							
5.							
6.							
7.							
8.							
9.							
10.							
11.							
12.							
13.							
14.							
15.							
16.							
17.							
18.							
19.							
20.							
Totals							

Total receivables (from financial statement)

$$\frac{\text{TOP 20 \$}}{\text{TOTAL REC.}} = \boxed{} \%$$

Taking Control Series Form # 32
1994 © The Merritt Company

What percentage do your top 20 receivables represent of your accounts receivable?

Are any of the customers on the list still buying on credit?

Do you have limits as to how much credit you will allow?

Are there trends that connect the type of customer and the amount of money owed?

Are there trends in the business or industry sector that connect the type of customer and the amount owed?

Are there economic factors that explain trends in receivables?

ANALYSIS OF CASH POSITION

This worksheet shows where money went besides paying for the expenses itemized in the Income Statement. A company made money but doesn't have cash to show for it. Why? Where did the cash go, and how much was used up by the operations, and how much was consumed by other things.

It will analyze where the company's cash comes from — and goes.

This worksheet is a variation of the accountant's Statement of Changes in Cash which is a required part of a publicly-traded company's financial reporting.

There are three areas of cash use shown in this worksheet:

- Cash used for operations — Cash flows from operating activities are generally the cash impact of changes in working capital accounts and from the basic operations of the company. Examples of increases to cash would include net income, collection of accounts receivables, decreases in inventory and depreciation. Examples of decreases to cash would include a net loss, increases in accounts receivable balances, increases in inventory, and payments of accounts payable.

- Cash used for investing activities (buying fixed assets, making acquisitions)

- Cash used for financing activities (repayment of bank debt, long-term leases)

Enter in the numbers called for both for the current month and year to date from your income statement (first line only) and from your balance sheet (remainder of the worksheet), and total the numbers in the shaded boxes to find your net increase or decrease in cash for the period.

Analysis of Cash Position

	Current Month	YTD
Operating Activities:		
Net Income/(Loss)		
Adjustments to Reconcile Net Income/Loss to Cash		
Depreciation & Amortization		
Changes in Assets & Liabilities--		
(Increase) Decrease in Accounts Receivable		
(Increase) Decrease in Inventory		
(Increase) Decrease in Prepaid Expenses		
(Increase) Decrease in Other Current Assets		
Increase (Decrease) in Accounts Payable		
Increase (Decrease) in Current Portion Long-Term Debt		
Increase (Decrease) in Accrued Liabilities		
Total Adjustments		
Net Cash Provided By (Used For) Operating Activities		
Investing Activities:		
Additions to Fixed Assets		
(Increase) Decrease in Other Assets		
Other		
Net Cash Provided By (Used For) Investing Activities		
Financing Activities:		
Line of Credit Borrowings (repayments)		
Principle Payments on Long-Term Debt		
Net Cash From (Used For) Financing Activities		
Net Increase (Decrease) In Cash For Period		
Cash @ Beginning of Period		
Cash @ End of Period		

Taking Control Series Form # 33
1994 © The Merritt Company

This is a complex worksheet. You may wish to get assistance from your CPA, especially if you have sales and fixed assets changes during the period.

Was there a net increase or decrease to your cash for the period? For the year?

Was the change from operational factors, investing factors, or financing factors?

Are there changes you can make to positively influence your cash position?

Is the company generating positive cash flow from operations?

If the company is losing money, how is that loss being financed? With new equity? With payables?

KEY FINANCIAL INDICATORS

Overview

This worksheet provides a one-page comparison of all of the key financial numbers comparing two years past to the current year.

Used well, it will give managers a broad view, over three years, of trends in their business that relate to cash.

I use this sheet at Board meetings and to give to employees to illustrate, in simple terms, how the company is doing. It is a communications tool for displaying analysis I've done in other worksheets and exercises.

Directions

Keep a running total on all of your major financial numbers — cash, revenue, expenses, and income — and enter the current month when available.

Record your accounts receivable and accounts payable days, as well as your total accounts receivable.

Questions to ask

Are the long-term trends (taking up the entire three years) what you want them to be?

Have expense increases outpaced revenue increases?

Are accounts receivable days and accounts payable days increasing or decreasing?

Are overdue accounts receivable increasing or decreasing?

Does this worksheet accurately display the financial strengths and weaknesses that your company has?

Key Financial Indicators

CASH

		Jan.	Feb.	March	April	May	June	July	Aug.	Sept.	Oct.	Nov.	Dec.
This year	Proj												
	Act												
Last year	Act												
Two years ago	Act												

Revenue

	Jan.	Feb.	March	April	May	June	July	Aug.	Sept.	Oct.	Nov.	Dec.
This year												
Last year												
Two years ago												

Expenses

		Jan.	Feb.	March	April	May	June	July	Aug.	Sept.	Oct.	Nov.	Dec.
This year	Proj												
	Act												
Last year	Act												
Two years ago	Act												

Income Month To Date & Year To Date

		Jan. MTD	YTD	Feb. MTD	YTD	March MTD	YTD	April MTD	YTD	May MTD	YTD	June MTD	YTD
This year	Proj												
	Act												
Last year	Act												
Two years ago	Act												

		July MTD	YTD	Aug. MTD	YTD	Sept. MTD	YTD	Oct. MTD	YTD	Nov. MTD	YTD	Dec. MTD	YTD
This year	Proj												
	Act												
Last year	Act												
Two years ago	Act												

Accounts Receivable Days

	Jan.	Feb.	March	April	May	June	July	Aug.	Sept.	Oct.	Nov.	Dec.
This year												
Last year												
Two years ago												

Accounts Payable Days

	Jan.	Feb.	March	April	May	June	July	Aug.	Sept.	Oct.	Nov.	Dec.
This year												
Last year												
Two years ago												

Accounts Receivable

	Jan.	Feb.	March	April	May	June	July	Aug.	Sept.	Oct.	Nov.	Dec.
CURRENT												
30+												
60+												
90+												
120+												
TOTAL												

Financial Report to Employees

Overview

This worksheet — also a communications tool — provides a simple way to keep employees informed about those key indicators upon which they can have an impact and help keep the company financially healthy.

Consider sending this worksheet and its attachments to all employees every month. In addition, have a monthly meeting to go over these numbers and answer questions about what they mean, and how they relate to each job done in the company.

Directions

Enter the numbers from the Key Financial Indicators worksheet for the current month as well as a running total for the year to date.

Provide a simple analysis at the bottom of the page by determining which of your key items is up or down and translating the importance of these items for your employees.

Attach the important financial worksheets developed in this section.

Questions to ask

Are you on target for where you expected to be at this point in the year?

Are there things employees can do to help your company reach its financial goals and projections?

Do employees understand the numbers and concepts presented in this worksheet? If not, how long will it take to teach them the things they need to know?

TO: All Employees

Financial Report to Employees
for _____
(month/year)

	Current Month	Prior Month	Two Months Ago	YTD
Sales				
Expenses:				
Cost of Goods Sold				
Gross Profit Margin				
Sales Expense				
Administration				
Total Expense				
Income (sales minus expense)				
Cash				
Inventory $:				
A/R Days:				
A/P Days:				
Inventory Turndays:				

Attachments:

1. Year at a Glance Income Statement

    Sales were (above/below) projections by x%

    Expenses were (over/under) budget by x%. Especially over budget were the following items:

2. Key Financial Indicators

    Profits were (above/below) projections by x%.

3. Analysis of Cash Position

    Our cash was (under/over) projections by x%.

Comments:

CHAPTER 5: MARKETING

No business factor irritates, perplexes and challenges owners and managers more than marketing — perhaps because the term covers so many activities and disciplines. In many companies it includes sales, customer research and elements of product development.

This confusion leads some managers away from giving sales and marketing the attention they deserve. Successful companies boast that they are "market responsive" or "market driven," but in truth, in a world that depends on information, all companies must be market responsive. Your customers don't buy your products or those of your competitors for mysterious reasons, and whether you make hardware for cars, disk drives for computers or movies for Hollywood, you must know who your customers are and what they want. You have to notice when their wants and needs change.

The Need for Information

Delivering better products faster and more efficiently to your customers requires lots of information. Marketing — in its broadest definition — is that information. It's a means of figuring out what works and doesn't work for your business.

This chapter takes you through this process by:

- Considering your industry sector's potential;
- Considering your competition;
- Compiling sales and customer data into meaningful categories;
- Determining dollar sales per customer;
- Reviewing marketing activities to date;
- Analyzing sales trends;

What works and what doesn't

The basics vary

- Assessing unit sales volume versus dollar sales volume; and

- Assessing dollar sales by product.

The basics of marketing vary greatly depending on the business. In publishing, for example, marketing entails huge expenses for advertising, publicity and distribution because selling books or data relies on thousands of small and sometimes impulsive transactions. Marketing in the defense industry, on the other hand, entails meeting new customers face-to-face and networking on Capitol Hill and in the Pentagon — because defense contracting relies on a few huge and lengthily considered transactions.

Whoever and wherever they are, your customers can get just about anything they want at any time they want it. They can get the things or services they want from you or from someone else, and usually on terms pretty close to their own. Consumers have become accustomed to getting products faster and better and with high quality service. In fact, products are generally sold on one or more of three criteria — quality, value (more useful concept than cost) and service. The challenge to your marketing efforts is to determine what combination of these basics works most effectively for the product you make.

You learn much from the people in the marketplace who love your products and even more from those who don't. This means taking a hard look at your successes and your failures.

Marketing Data

A good marketing plan helps you diagnose and solve any problems related to the external factors that affect your sales — for example, a widespread recession. California-based marketing consultant Molly Thorpe reports that during the recession of the early 1990s, nine out of ten of her clients focused their marketing efforts on boosting profitability rather than increasing revenues against the economic currents.

According to Thorpe, most companies use marketing information weakly and ineffectively. "Many businesses don't focus on who their real customers are because they are afraid to turn away business," she says. "But it's important to identify who you don't want to sell to, so you don't squander your resources."

To do this, you need good information about your sales and customers, the industry sectors to which you sell and your competition. It is important to chart the information about sales and customers through time by week, month, or year, by product type, by location, by customer type, by marketing method, by dollar volume, and any other way that fits with your business.

Constructing a matrix — a graphic structure that gives form to disparate pieces of information — allows you to illustrate the information you've collected. This helps you look at the information from a variety of perspectives — upside down and sideways, friendly and antagonistic.

Critical Information

When you complete the worksheets and exercises in this section, you should be able to put together a series of marketing matrices capturing critical data in a form that will make its significance clear.

To do these worksheets and exercises, you need to list:

- Your customers by name, by product purchased, by type, by location;

- Dollar sales by month, by product;

- Unit sales by month, by product;

- Dollar sales by method of marketing (advertising, direct mail, etc.);

- Dollar sales from new business versus repeat business, by product; and

- Dollars spent on marketing, by method of marketing.

As we noted in Chapter 4, financial analysis trails sales. Here we see that marketing precedes sales. Finance entails fundamentally — if not exclusively

Good data on your customers

183

The nature of marketing

— quantitative activities. Marketing entails fundamentally qualitative activities. Marketing consultants may support their advice (and billable hours) with columns of numbers, but in its simplest form marketing is a series of intuitive decisions full of value judgments about what will succeed in a given place at a given time. Even the language of marketing — perceived value compared to cost, high effectiveness, clear message to customers, high market penetration, customer satisfaction (some marketing experts prefer the more assertive term "customer delight") — gives away the qualitative nature of the work.

Leading the Marketplace

Sometimes, in making those judgments, you go against the advice of people you respect — and convince them only after the fact. Saloom Furniture Company, a Massachusetts-based manufacturer of quality furniture sold through retail outlets, saw potential in making tables with tops of Dupont Corian, a composite that looks like marble. When Saloom asked its retailers about the idea, the retailers didn't think they'd sell because consumers didn't know about Corian. They said it sounded cheap and cost too much. Saloom didn't follow this advice, and its Corian tables became big sellers.

Peter and Linda Saloom started the company in 1981, as Peter Saloom's interest in furniture making progressed from a hobby to a business. In 1986, with revenues of $300,000, the business moved into a small mill and the Salooms hired their first employees.

The company had gone without a business plan until that point. But to move into the mill, the Salooms needed financing, and the banks wanted a plan. The Salooms put one together and got the loans they needed, but that only started a long process. "The toughest part is going from plan to implementation — having the discipline required to go through the necessary steps to communicate to make sure there is a comprehensive understanding," Peter Saloom says. "It is a very time consuming process. And you're not making furniture while you're making plans."

The Salooms focus their plans on the short term, only one or two years at a time. "Toward the end of each year, the management team talks to their departments," Linda Saloom says, to determine how to accomplish their goals. "Then we have weekly meetings where all the managers come together. We look at implementation. If there seems to be a problem, we address it."

This is a top-down process. Some employees complain, since the company in other ways encourages employee involvement. But the Salooms believe that implementation has to stay tightly focused.

"We set a goal and try to make it tangible and accessible. Quality index rating and specific targets and benchmarks tell us if everything is going great or not," Peter Saloom says. Then, in the day-to-day implementation, there's room for more response. "You look for response. When employees can say what they have to do and how to do it, then you know you've communicated your objectives."

But these objectives frequently conflict. For example, keeping quality high sometimes interferes with deadlines. "We rate these things against each other," Peter Saloom says, "so there's a hierarchy of objectives. Our first goal: work safely. Our next goal: maintain quality. Next: deliver on time. Next: lower cost. If somebody's safety measure is bad, we don't care about how quick they are."

Regular Review

The Salooms also work hard to monitor performance. "You need to look at a number of things on a regular basis," Linda Saloom says. "We receive our P&L that we review every month. We know these numbers and how high they are over a number of years . . . Knowledge of what a cost is and what the trend is, that's important. One of the best things to improve cost is to improve quality. Why do we have returns? Are we collecting our money fast, slow or the same?"

From the top down

'An edge in the market'

The Salooms don't obsess on monitoring financial performance. They try to use their financials as tools. "Numbers are important, but if I lost my employees tomorrow it wouldn't matter what the numbers were. If you want an up and going company, you want people who are motivated. Their commitments, their motivations, their pride in their work—that's what will generate numbers," Linda Saloom says. As a result, "we're not budgeters. We think budgets actually increase costs. If money is allotted to something, it will usually be spent."

Saloom Furniture is "not a heavily marketing-oriented company," either, but the Salooms think about their market pragmatically.

"We resist jumping into hot products. When something's already hot, it means it's a highly competitive market. What you try to do is avoid the competition. You try to be the leader because it gives you an edge in the market," Peter Saloom says. "You have to listen to your customers but you have to synthesize what they are telling you in a more original interpretation."

The company proved the value of this advice in bringing its Corian tables to market. By 1992, the company had revenues of $7.5 million and more than 30 employees. Saloom Furniture makes about 4,000 chairs and 800 to 900 tables a month, mostly custom-built to consumer specifications. In 1993, Peter and Linda Saloom were named Small Business Persons of the Year in Massachusetts.

External Forces

It's easy to pose the questions you want to answer about your market and your competitors—and difficult to answer them. Managers must do more with less when looking outside the organization for factors influencing sales. Among the most important of these questions:

- What is your position in your industry?
- What are the sales and profit trends in your sector?

- What are the product trends? What's hot? What's cold?

- How do you expect your industry to change in the next year? In the next five years?

- What are the strengths and weaknesses of your competitors's products? Of their management teams?

- How do they mix quality, value and service?

- Can you bring new products to market more quickly than your competitors?

Begin your market research by asking everyone in your company to write down everything they know about your competition and its products. From this, expect to pull a variety of impressions; your sales staff will probably have a different perspective than your technical people. The object is to build a universe within which you can place and define your product and how your customers perceive you. You want to understand your competition so as to differentiate your product.

Knowing your marketplace has a direct impact on what you do. A management consultant from the Midwest tells the story of an inventor with little marketing experience who invented a new toy — a great product combining mechanical simplicity with endless variations in outcome. The excited inventor couldn't wait to bring his product to market.

The problem: He wasn't sure what — or where — that market was.

He needed a partner who knew toy marketing. He found one, but the partner didn't understand the appeal of the inventor's toy. Instead, the marketer came to the deal with a load of preconceived notions about how to sell consumer products that didn't fit the product. The partners failed to get the toy on retail shelves or create word-of-mouth publicity. They sold through mail order catalogues, but the toy didn't take off with consumers.

Clear idea of the market

Several years and one partnership later, the inventor had to start over, taking the time to learn how a tightknit industry like children's toys works and what one must do to get a product recognized.

A Solid Plan

Unlike this inventor, Jeffrey Schmidt and Clark Greenlee, who started a successful espresso bar in the Country Club shopping district of Kansas City, had a clear eye on their market when they started out.

Working as architects in Washington, D.C. they saw running an espresso bar as a good way to put their design skills to practical use. Coffee bars had proliferated in Washington, and Schmidt figured that Kansas City, his home town, might prove a good market for a business relying heavily on atmosphere and inexpensive extravagance.

He and Greenlee did some basic market research. They went to espresso bars whenever they had the chance. They enrolled in Small Business Administration classes on starting a business and writing business plans. They contacted officials in Kansas City.

In 1991, Schmidt started scouting locations. He focused on the Country Club Plaza, a shopping and business district south of downtown with good foot traffic — essential for an espresso bar.

He contacted J.C. Nichols Co., the big real estate management firm that runs the Country Club district. Nichols liked the concept and asked to see a business plan.

Their Own Strengths

It took them three months to put one together. The plan reflected Schmidt and Greenlee's strengths in architecture. It forecast sales and cash flow and analyzed the Kansas City marketplace and the performance of analogous cafes and restaurants. Schmidt and Greenlee projected that they could do well if they sold 400 cups of espresso a day. That figure seemed in line with comparable shops in comparable markets.

Nichols had seen other pitches from people who wanted to start espresso bars in the Country Club Plaza. It chose Schmidt and Greenlee because they best understood the market for an upscale coffee place.

With the landlord on their side, Schmidt and Greenlee began meeting with bankers in Kansas City. Between them, the partners had $30,000 to invest. United Missouri Bank lent them another $70,000 under an SBA program.

"They had a great business plan, they came in and presented it very well and they seemed sharp and on the ball, qualities we look for in a borrower," said the bank officer who made the loan.

With financing arranged, Schmidt and Greenlee signed a lease with Nichols for a prime spot in the Country Club Plaza. The partners started a crash course in managing espresso bars; Greenlee worked at a successful outlet back in Washington. They lined up contractors and permits and polished their designs for the store, knowing that the look would play a key role in its success. Throughout, Schmidt and Greenlee showed their knowledge of their customers — young urbanites seeking attractive places to spend time.

The shop opened in spring 1993. By the end of the year, it had become one of the most thriving locations in the Country Club Plaza. Sales ran 50 percent ahead of projections and the place already turned a healthy profit.

The Customer

Once you analyze your product from the perspective of the competition and the marketplace, you move to the most important factor — your customer.

Bill Miller, a project manager with the Price Waterhouse marketing consulting group Management Horizons, sees four essentials in a marketing plan:

- Define your audience and product purpose;
- Focus on specific values you provide to the customer;

Using focus groups

- Do your homework — the research to support your conclusions;
- Remember that marketing should always lead to some sort of sale.

Ask people whose opinions you respect to review your plans with an objective eye. These people don't have to be experts in your industry.

Miller's group works primarily in the retail merchandise industry with clients like Sears, Pier One Imports, the Warner Brothers and Disney store chains, and the Limited — a sector with complex customer and product mixes.

Retailers use benchmarks, but Miller says that making generalizations about which benchmarks to use can be dangerous. "The benchmarks you'll use will vary too much by product and industry," he says.

Management Horizons distributes questionnaires, surveys individual customers, convenes focus groups and interviews people about their buying habits, what they look for in clothes and other products, where and why they go first when they enter a store.

Watch and Listen

You don't have to hire a consultant to do this research. Draw your focus groups from selected markets and targeted customers. Attract these groups with small amounts of cash or sample products. In the interview, describe a product or service — or, better yet, show them — and ask for feedback. Watch as well as listen to the reaction.

Don't look to focus groups for answers or specific guidance. Even if the group is large — a dozen people — it can't give you reliable answers about market conditions.

But review the results of focus groups with as many managers as feasible. This educates your staff about the problems the product will face — and gives your company the chance to respond. Staff needs to see customers talking about what they want. Seeing this response arouses the attention, making innovation more likely.

Set up interviews by phone, mail or in person with targeted customers. Find out how these customers consider quality, value and service in relation to your product. Ask them to describe their responses in some detail.

Look for information on price ranges and barriers, format or style preferences, service requirements, probable buying patterns.

Find out how customers perceive your competition. Another point to explore: How do your customers get information about competitors and their products — advertising, direct mail, word of mouth?

Consider the factors beyond your control that affect your customers — geographic boundaries, demographic limits and cultural influences. Some marketing consultants ignore these factors as beyond your control. That's a mistake. You can still observe them and react accordingly.

Analyze the responses with a focus on what features your product should have and what would make it more attractive. Find out where you outperform or lag your competition. The objective: To inform your sales force how to move units.

Illustrate your results in graphic form and publicize them within your company. Let your coworkers know what customers think of their work and what they look for in the future.

Customer research seeks to learn what motivates people to buy what you sell. In this process, anything that tracks sales in a detailed way helps you — a major reason why big retailers offer their own credit cards, encourage catalog orders, and code their register receipts. It's also why direct mail marketers offer free gifts, and why home shopping and computer on-line services make marketers' mouths water.

You can't control marketplace forces, but you can minimize your marketing risks. When you own a reliable base of data about your customers and their tendencies, you can sell selectively to people most

Track the details

The market is king

likely to buy a particular product. If you know that middle aged Philadelphia men buy red ties in February, you know all you need to know.

Playing a Tough Field

Colorado-based SPA Inc. sells what it calls "environmentally conscious" cosmetics into the retail market. Co-founder John Schoenauer argues that the market for his product is sophisticated and well developed, not trendy, and that SPA must pay close attention to its market in order to survive.

He targets upscale women 20 to 40 years old. The company identifies customers by buying patterns, income, product orientation and location. "We identified a market niche already sensitive to environmental products. We're trying to take advantage of an overall awareness among American consumers at this point," Schoenauer says.

SPA's products cost about half the price of comparable department store products and come with a money-back guarantee. The company has consumer research that bears out its claims that people rate its product quality highly.

Making environmentally conscious products entails some added costs. Natural ingredients cost more than synthetics. Chemists take longer to work with them, often mixing several natural ingredients to achieve results yielded by a single synthetic.

Then there are the huge marketing and advertising costs of the cosmetics business. Giants like Estee Lauder spend 60 to 70 percent of retail unit price on marketing, starting with display ads in fashion magazines and ending in promotional specials in department stores.

Low Costs, Prices

SPA doesn't spend that kind of money. Schoenauer says the company "starts from bottom up," analyzing costs and determining a reasonable profit margin. Then it targets prices based on those numbers.

"In our case, we're priced so far below our competitors that consumers are amazed they're not paying more. If I were more astute I'd probably raise the prices," Schoenauer laughs. SPA's philosophy: honest products at honest prices.

But marketing remains key. The cosmetics industry posts more than $20 billion in annual revenues. Within this universe, "natural product" cosmetics account for about $500 million.

"There's no legal definition for natural," Schoenauer says. "The only thing the FDA looks at are claims you make. Some companies will have one natural ingredient and 17 others synthetic — and they'll call the products natural."

In one sense it doesn't matter how loosely you define the term. As a marketer, SPA competes with all cosmetic companies from the wholly natural to the devoutly synthetic, including Body Shop, Garden Botanic, H20 Plus and Bath & Body Works.

"Hardly anybody in our natural category advertises. They choose to position locally to get a lot of walk-by traffic," Schoenauer says. That's why a start-up company like SPA had a chance. "Still, as a small underfunded company, it's difficult," he says. "One strategy is to go into secondary markets. To support our pricing philosophy, we don't want to go into upscale malls where four other people are selling the same product. We're not wealthy enough to pour hundreds of thousands of dollars into enticing customers."

Second-Tier Markets

Schoenauer says that focusing on second-tier markets — what the company calls "metropolitan mid-America" — worked well for Wal-Mart. SPA can dominate smaller markets by bringing big-market trends to the masses, and it doesn't slug it out with dozens of competitors in New York and Los Angeles.

The company owns three stores in Denver and licenses others in Colorado and the Midwest. Following the business plan he wrote almost ten years ago, Schoenauer intends to expand by licensing new stores. SPA doesn't charge an up-front fee or impose a royalty structure. It wants simply to sell product, which licensees resell. For a company still trying to

Asking the right questions

establish its brand name, this kind of deal attracts more interest.

In dealing with licensees, Schoenauer has had to scrutinize his original business plan to develop a financial model to attract investors in new stores. The model explains the licensing deal, the investment required, the inventory terms, company philosophy and the products themselves.

Schoenauer keeps his business plan under wraps; he says the cosmetics industry is too competitive. "Anyone who sees the plan must sign a release promising not to discuss any of its details. It's the only way to protect our business," he says.

But Schoenauer does talk about the company's approach to marketing.

"We are manufacturers avoiding lots of distribution costs by going directly into licensing stores," he says. "We think there's a huge market for these stores, particularly among women who'd like to own their own business in this kind of market. When the cosmetics industry and the environmental movement meet, you can bet that big dollars are not far behind."

The Details

Sales are the best tool for measuring the effectiveness of your marketing, but they don't tell you everything you need to know. If sales increase, you're doing something right. But it sometimes takes some digging to find out what. You want to make the best and most effective use of your sales resources, and you need to analyze your numbers so that you know what "best" and "most effective" mean.

This includes looking for the highest margin. Find out what the average gross profit margin is for your industry and market and see whether you expect to outdo or fall below the standard — and whether you can stay in business at that margin.

But profit isn't everything, especially when you undertake a long term marketing program. Such a program might call for you to cultivate satisfied customers who believe they get their money's worth and will come back a second and third time. This may require you to sacrifice short term profitability — a good sacrifice if you like your chances over the long term.

Your marketing people help here by tracking your revenues so that you know what kind of sales work the best. The cliche holds that 80 percent of a company's sales come from 20 percent of its customers, and whatever numbers apply to you, the message remains that your sales numbers tell you a lot about your business.

You just have to ask the right questions.

Different companies bring different priorities to this analysis, depending on their goals. We analyze them from the standpoint of the growth-oriented company pursuing those sales most likely to have the highest average dollar volume. Six of the worksheets in this section bring this into focus, analyzing:

- Top 25 dollar-volume customers;
- Top selling products;
- Sales by product and customer, year-to-year;
- Sales by product and marketing method;
- Dollar sales comparisons month-to-month, by product;
- Unit sales comparisons month-to-month, by product.

Thorough Preparations

Taken together, these worksheets go a long way toward identifying who does business with you and why. In turn, this information prepares you to make the best and most effective use of your marketing and sales efforts — as Ruth Owades showed in establishing an upscale catalog marketer of flowers and plants, California-based Calyx & Corolla, Inc., in 1988.

Calyx & Corolla succeeded quickly because of the strong planning that Owades brought to the venture. She had worked in the mail-order and catalog

The best effort

'The logic of the business'

business for more than a decade. Her first venture in catalog marketing, in the 1970s, was a company called Gardener's Eden, which sold quality gardening tools and supplies. She sold Gardener's Eden to a big East Coast catalog company. The experience gave her contacts and expertise in direct-mail marketing.

The idea of selling flowers and plants through the mail attracted her. The flower industry seemed ripe for innovation, and the mail-order business remained popular.

Researching the competition, Owades found several futile attempts at selling flowers through catalogs, most engineered by flower cooperatives with no feel for catalog sales.

Owades knew the catalog business well, had some money and committed to developing her idea.

"I wanted to start big; with so many people watching us, the risk of competition was sizable," she told one interviewer. "If it was going to work, we really had to carve out a niche quickly and establish ourselves."

She needed $2 million in startup capital and set a goal of $3 to $4 million in revenue during Calyx & Corolla's second year of operations. She read up on writing business plans and developed her own — discovering, as she puts it, that writing a plan "uncovered the logic of the business." She put $150,000 of her own money into the company and tried something that might have seemed gimmicky — or, worse, might not have worked at all. She sent potential investors flowers via Federal Express, just as Calyx & Corolla customers would receive them.

Her business plan, her commitment and her Fed Ex flowers worked. Within a few weeks, she lined up all the money she needed. She hadn't done much direct market research, betting $2 million that her ideas and her experience would make the project work. She felt confident that Calyx & Corolla could sell flowers in the $50 price range with a guarantee of overnight delivery. But she wasn't sure whether people would order flowers from a catalog instead of a flower shop.

Tough Sales

In many ways, catalog sales are among the most difficult to close. Catalog shoppers usually compare products and prices carefully — and slowly. The impulse purchases that drive discretionary sales like flowers rarely play a big role in catalog marketing. But Owades knew that high-income people, especially women, shop extensively by catalog. She had no problem seeing her ideal customer — someone much like herself.

So she knew that her catalog would play a pivotal role in the company's success. She called on all of her experience to lend the catalog a sense of affluence and elegance. She wanted customers to believe Calyx & Corolla had been around forever.

She intended to process orders in San Francisco. The flowers would go directly from growers to customers via overnight delivery — so the company's success depended on good relations with growers and shippers.

Handling things with growers was easy. Owades found many growers looking for new ways to package product. She had no problem selling them on the idea of catalog sales.

Finding the right delivery system proved more difficult. "Because of the reputation and stature it would give our business, I felt my shipper had to be Federal Express," Owades has said. "Airborne, Emery, and a variety of others were eager to have the business and were competitive on price but could not promise the lift capacity, the airplane space out of specific locations and a guarantee on a day-in, day-out basis to move product."

She showed good timing. Federal Express had recently made courting small businesses like Calyx & Corolla a priority. Owades set up an account with Fed Ex that assured her of on-time delivery to almost any spot in the continental U.S.

Effective Catalog

She was ready. Her first catalog went out in January 1989, and it did its job. Orders came in above

New
ways
to
package
product

What the customer values

Owades' projections. In 1992, its fourth year in business, the company generated profits exceeding 5 percent on sales of $10 million.

Since starting the company, Owades has raised another $1 million from her original investors. She still worries about communicating her concept to people who aren't used to buying things through catalogs, but she believes in the catalog as a marketing vehicle. And she believes that Calyx & Corolla will eventually show revenues of $100 million.

The Quality Sale

In retail sales, marketing consultants check every aspect of the business from the design of the store to lighting to display to the look of the clerks. Bill Miller, the consultant with Business Horizons, points out that stores in the Gap and Limited chains are very clean not because managers enforce personal manias for cleanliness but because market research indicates that customers put a big value on clean stores.

We all know of companies that balance customer needs with their own growth and profit objectives. These success stories don't happen by accident. The companies look for sales that generate the most money for the longest time — quality sales.

You find the quality sale by investigating your marketing methods, using the worksheets in this chapter. If you have an in-house sales force and also use outside representatives, compare the cost-effectiveness of the two methods. Likewise, if you use wholesale distributors and direct mail, make sure you know which sales come from which operation, and find out why. What you come up with points to the quality sale — and to how to get more such sales.

Most sales are based equally on belief in a product and trust in the person selling it. People do business with people, not demographic surveys. Customers want to — and have to — believe in what and from whom they're buying. You have a lot of control over whether they believe.

Many managers find that good service is a key to

quality sales, and studies of consumer and corporate buying habits consistently reinforce the idea. In some markets, customers rate service more highly than quality in choosing one product over another.

Good marketing tells you how well you serve your customers by collecting information and adapting this knowledge to your markets. It:

- Identifies and defines customer expectations regarding service;

- Translates expectations into clear, deliverable service features;

- Arranges efficient, responsive, and integrated service delivery systems and structures;

- Monitors and controls service quality and performance; and,

- Provides quick, cost-effective response to customers' needs.

Marketing creates sales opportunities. If, for example, you enhance your product's usefulness to your customer by offering valuable benefits from a related line, you create an interested listener ready to hear more about your products. Each time you propose an innovative approach to a real need, you create a sales opportunity. In order to do these things, your sales force has to know how customers use your products.

To gauge this effectiveness, you need to measure how your sales force responds to different marketing methods. This is similar to — but not exactly the same as — monitoring sales by marketing method.

The manner in which you structure your sales force's commission schedule can work against marketing efforts, if you don't pay attention. The best way to avoid trouble in this regard is to budget percentages of sale price to sales and marketing. This way, when the cost of a marketing method is high, you keep commissions low.

The Bottom Line

Like operations, marketing brings a particular per-

Looking for future sales

spective — and particular priorities — to management. Unchecked, its impulse for growth and innovation can hurt you. If you ever have doubts about allocating resources, err toward making sure that your marketing efforts remain profitable.

However you monitor its effectiveness, your marketing department should seek to remove the barriers blocking communication between you and your customers. This usually takes the form of research and information-gathering. But whatever form it takes, it needs to focus on two objectives: simplicity and sales.

Your marketing goals should seek to:

- Increase the number of potential customers who come into contact with you;

- Increase your conversion rate, so that more of these potential customers actually buy from you; and

- Make sure they buy again.

Because small companies often depend on a few loyal customers to stay in business, some managers tend to pursue those sales at all costs. But marketing efforts look for future sales; they don't value existing business simply because it exists.

Other managers become so enamored of the forward-looking spin of good marketing has that they ignore all else. "A lot of people don't really want to be the president. They want to be the marketing guy," says one Maryland-based consultant.

INDUSTRY QUESTIONNAIRE

This questionnaire assesses the market opportunities in the industries and markets your company serves.

Industry information may give you an idea about what your market share is. It may also tell you where developing new products may be most beneficial.

Overview

Fill out one of these for each industry in which you provide products or services at least annually.

Sources of industry information include trade associations, the U.S. Commerce Department, Standard & Poor's Industry Report, Dun & Bradstreet (many of these can be found in local libraries), annual reports of publicly held companies, on-line data services such as Nexis and Dow Jones, news services, and by talking to industry experts.

Directions

Is this an industry that offers opportunities for your company now and in the future?

Are there significant barriers to growth in this industry?

Are your sales and marketing strategies focused on the right type of consumer in this kind of market sector?

Does your market reward broad-based efforts or niche operations?

What can you do to position the company for growth that takes advantage of its market and industry sectors? If growth prospects are limited, should you consider moving out of that market?

Questions to ask

Industry Questionnaire

1. Total buying power:

   _____ number of buyers

   _____ estimated $ buying volume

2. Is this a "mature" or start-up industry?

3. What are the barriers, if any, to entry in the industry?

4. Who are the industry leaders, why?

5. How many companies operate in this industry? Is the number increasing or declining?

6. Can your company expand the market in this industry?

7. Are there particular demographic factors at work in this industry?

8. Are there seasonal buying patterns inherent to this industry?

9. Can you find projections of growth trends for the industry (projections done by trade groups, security analysts, government)?

10. What are the factors that will affect demand for your product (general business conditions, technological innovation, governmental factors, customer growth)?

11. Are there any potentially adverse political, social, economic, or environmental conditions?

Assessment of Competition

This worksheet provides a means to keep track of competitors' progress in the market and to learn from their successes and failures.

Being able to anticipate how a competitor will act or react can provide a significant advantage in planning your strategy.

Keeping track of your competition is more important as a sales tool than as a means of setting goals for product development or service. It is important to know what they do well, because your customers will know, even if you don't.

List all the major competitors you know about. Use industry magazines, or trade association contacts, financial reports (like those mentioned in the Industry Questionnaire section) or news services. Some entrepreneurs even telephone competitors directly to find out about their sales volume, products, and pricing policies.

Obtain their catalogs or other marketing materials, and buy their products or use their services. Ask friends what they like and don't like about the competitors' product.

After reviewing publicly available data on competitors, prepare this detailed assessment of the competition. This assessment will help identify competitors' strengths and weaknesses in products, quality, service, price, etc.

Assessment of Competition

Competitor's Name: **Location:**

Parent Company: ☐ **Subsidiary**   ☐ **Division**   ☐ **Branch**

Product Lines(s):

	Sales	Net Income	Total Assets	Equity
19____				
19____				
19____				

Estimated Market Share

Rate the following areas in order to determine major strengths and weaknesses of the competitor (suggest using "+", "N", "—"):

1. **Name recognition**   _____

2. **Product line**   _____

3. **Quality**   _____

4. **New products**   _____

5. **Pricing**   _____

6. **Marketing share**   _____

7. **Financial condition**   _____

"+" Better than your company
"N" Neutral — about the same as your company
"—" Worse than your company

Briefly describe the competitor's reputation, competitive advantages and disadvantages and overall marketing strategy:

Taking Control Series Form # 38
1994 © The Merritt Company

Can you counter each competitor's weakness with a strength in your product or service? How else can you turn their weaknesses to your advantage?

Could they counter your weaknesses with their strengths?

What parts of the market is your competition moving into? Moving away from? Do these trends have any bearing on your business?

Are your competitors more stable and better-capitalized than you are? Does this matter much in your market?

How does your company's market position compare to those of your competitors? Are you a market leader or a market follower? Is there an advantage to being one or the other (which makes more money)?

Dollar Sales Month to Month

This is a simple and straightforward way to look at what your actual sales are month by month, compared to projections, by product. A lot of information is contained in a very simple worksheet.

This enables you, much better than an overall sales summary for the company, to see what is working and what isn't. For which products sales are steadily increasing, and which products may need changes in direction to remain viable.

The worksheet shows actual sales figures compared to sales projections by month and determines average sales by month.

List all of your products, or product lines in the left column. Take the projections developed in the Dollar Sales Projections by Product worksheet, and add those in the second column.

Then, on a monthly basis, add in your actual sales dollars by product.

If you have records of past years, make copies of these worksheets, and plot the numbers for these years. Total all sales by month and put that number in the total column which is next to last. Finally, divide this number by the total number of months for which you have sales figures (divide by 12 if you have numbers for the whole year) to get an average dollar sales figure by month.

Dollar Sales Month To Month For _____
(Month/Year)

Product	Goal for Current Mo.	1 Jan.	2 Feb.	3 Mar.	4 April	5 May	6 June	7 July	8 Aug.	9 Sept.	10 Oct.	11 Nov.	12 Dec.	Total Year-to-date Sales	Avg. Sales by Mo.[1]
Totals															

[1] Divide total year-to-date Sales By Current Month number.

Taking Control Series Form # 39
1994 © The Merritt Company

Do you see any cyclicality by product?

Can you structure your sales and marketing efforts to take advantage of sales trends?

For which products are your goals more than your actual sales?

Is this because you were overly optimistic when making projections?

For which products do actual sales exceed goals? Is this expected to continue, or is it due to a particular marketing effort?

Product Sales by Customer

A goal of every company should be to sell as much of each type of product as possible to every customer it acquires. This calculation is an indication of how many dollars each customer spends with your company. Looking at three years of data lets you see whether customers are spending more on average than they did two years ago, or less.

Since so much money is spent just letting potential customers know that you exist, additional sales to existing customers are very profitable business. Every company should have a plan to sell more product to existing customers this worksheet can help you track if it is working.

It calculates your dollar volume per customer over the past three years.

Use the same three-year lists of products and total dollars per product you developed in the Dollar Sales Month to Month worksheet for the first two columns (A and B) of this worksheet.

Add the total number of customers that buy each product as column C.

Divide column B numbers by column C numbers to get column D.

Was this exercise difficult because so many customers buy more than one product or product type, or are your customers generally customers for one type of product only? (If you had a difficult time segregating customers by product, then the total company numbers at the bottom of the page will be most meaningful for you.)

Which products bring in the highest dollar volume per customer?

Product Sales By Customer

A Product	Two Years Ago			Last Year			This Year		
	B $ Sales	C # of Customers	D $ Per Customer (B ÷ C)	B $ Sales	C # of Customers	D $ Per Customer (B ÷ C)	B $ Sales	C # of Customers	D $ Per Customer (B ÷ C)
Total Company									

Taking Control Series Form # 40
1994 © The Merritt Company

In which products are the dollar volume per customer numbers going up each year?

Are these increases due to price fluctuation, or has the number of units sold to each of these customers gone up? (The shaded box in the very bottom right of the worksheet becomes one of your key indicators. Measured over time, this will tell you if you are increasing sales dollars per customer.)

Is your customer base shrinking or increasing?

Do a few customers account for a specific portion of a particular product's sales? If so, what can you do take optimum advantage of that connection?

Product Sales
by Marketing Method

Marketing a product often costs more than the manufacture of the product itself. Ineffective marketing efforts result in failed products, even if the products themselves meet every other criteria for product success.

To spend marketing dollars most effectively, the company must know what works, spend its money on things that work, or eliminate or modify efforts that are less successful. This is a constant process — a marketing method that has worked for years may decline, another type of effort may suddenly become more important.

To this end, it's important to determine not only what the sales were by product, but also which of the company's sales efforts made the customer aware of the product, decide to order it, and place an order by phone, mail, or in person, to the company directly, or through one of its other distribution channels.

Most companies use a variety of marketing methods. This worksheet lists many of them across the top. To begin, list your products and the total dollar volume sales attributed to each in the first and last columns on the sheet. Then determine how much of your business is new and how much is from customers who have done business with you before.

All of the new business should be broken down into how the customer first heard about you: by mail pieces you sent out, through the phone book, from telemarketing, from an advertisement(television, radio, or print media), through someone who sells for you (such as a retail establishment), through one of your sales reps, from word of mouth from another satisfied customer, or from some other channel.

Overview

Directions

Product Sales By Marketing Method
(last full year)

Product	Direct Mail	Telephone Book	Tele-marketing	Advertising	Distributors	Sales Force	Referral	Other	A New Sale Total	B Repeat Business	Total¹ Sales (A + B)
TOTALS											

New Sales $ (% of total sales) | ($/%) | (% of total sale)

¹The total by product comes from the $ sales column of the *Sales By Product and Customer* worksheet for last year

Taking Control Series Form # 41
1994 © The Merritt Company

In the top left portion of the box, list the actual dollars attributed to that type of marketing.

Once all the boxes are filled in, use the bottom right corner of the box to calculate the percentage of business attributed to that effort by dividing the total sales by effort by the new sales total.

Is one type of marketing responsible for most of your sales dollars? In total or just in one type of product?

Is this because your marketing expertise is limited, or because you've tried other methods and this is the one that works?

Are most methods of marketing represented to some extent, or are many boxes blank?

Could you use other marketing methods that you aren't currently using?

Is a disproportionate amount of your business either repeat or new? (You may be missing new opportunities if it is mostly repeat. However, if it is mostly new, it may mean that customers are not satisfied enough to return.)

Questions to ask

TOP 25 DOLLAR-VOLUME CUSTOMERS

Overview

This worksheet determines who are the customers that purchase the most dollar volume for this year and last year.

It is often useful to ask whether the types of people who buy from you have anything in common. Grouping types of customers will allow you to do this. Look at this worksheet for interesting patterns in customer type. For instance, your customers may be demographically similar: of a certain age, a particular income range, more men than women, etc. Or they may be similar in the business that they are affiliated with.

Location is important for the same reason. There may be something about your product that is particularly appealing to people in cities, or in warmer climates, or in newly developing areas.

Directions

Assemble a list of all of your customers for the past two years, and rank order the top 25 each year by dollar volume purchased.

On this worksheet, list your top customers starting with the customers who did the most business with you this year. List your most significant customers, even if you have fewer than 25. If you try to keep more than 25 customers on the list, it usually starts to get difficult hard to analyze effectively.

Also list the various types of customer you serve (if you have any statistics like SIC codes that segregate customers in meaningful ways) and their location (possibly by city, state, or zip code).

Top 25 Dollar-Volume Customers
(ranked by $ Volume)

Name	Customer Type	Location	$ Volume This Year	$ Volume/Ranking Last Year
1.				
2.				
3.				
4.				
5.				
6.				
7.				
8.				
9.				
10.				
11.				
12.				
13.				
14.				
15.				
16.				
17.				
18.				
19.				
20.				
21.				
22.				
23.				
24.				
25.				

Taking Control Series Form # 42
1994 © The Merritt Company

How significant is this group of customers to your business? To find out, first divide the total at the bottom of this page that adds up the sales volume of your top customers by the total sales of the company for that same period of time.

This group of customers accounted for _____ percent of the company's total sales.

Secondly, divide the number of significant customers you listed on this page with your total number of customers.

This group of customers makes up _____ percent of the company's total customer base.

Are your most significant customers mostly made up of a particular customer type?

If so, can you find ways to sell to more of these individuals?

Are your most significant customers centered in a particular location?

If so, can you find ways to market more heavily in this area?

Are you retaining your top dollar volume customers over time?

Are you acquiring new significant customers?

Top Selling Products

Overview

This exercise helps you determine which products sell the highest number of units and bring in the most revenue.

If you have only one product, this will be easy. If you have more than one, it is important to know which ones your customers like best. But even if you only have five, your top product is probably the one you should consider adding to with add-on or similar products.

You may also wish to analyze how you market these successful sellers and see if you can make similar efforts with other products.

Directions

Assemble a list of the sales in units and dollars of your products for the past two years. Rank them from top to bottom on the worksheet, starting with the product that sold the greatest dollar volume last year.

Complete the worksheet by filling in the projected and actual units and dollars for the two-year period.

Questions to ask

For which products were your actual numbers above or below your projections? Which caused the variances: the projections or your performance?

For which products did your sales volume increase? Why?

For which did it decrease? Why?

Do the trends up or down in sales suggest long-term changes in your market? Or can they be explained by circumstances within your company?

Are your top products related in any way? Could you create further products related to these? Could you market other products with these?

Top Selling Products

Product	Last Year				This Year			
	Units		Dollars		Units		Dollars	
	Projected	Actual	Projected	Actual	Projected	Actual	Projected	Actual
Totals:								

SALES REPORT TO EMPLOYEES

Overview

This worksheet — a communications tool — provides employees with a way to look at sales and receive an analysis meaningful to them about what the numbers mean.

Use this form as you would the Financial Report to Employees. Circulate it once a month and discuss it at regular meetings. You can use this report as an opportunity to congratulate outstanding performers on the sales team and encourage everyone to get involved in sales and promotion.

Directions

Fill in this worksheet with information from the Dollar Sales Month to Month worksheet and others in this section.

Provide a simple analysis at the bottom of the page by determining which products are up or down from projections and translating the importance of these changes for your employees.

Attach the important worksheets developed in this section.

Questions to ask

Are you where you expected to be in sales for the company overall, on a year-to-date basis?

Are some products doing much better than expected? Why?

Are some products behind expectations?

Are there reasons that can be corrected?

What can each employee focus on to improve sales?

Do employees understand the marketing concepts and numbers used in this report? If not, how long would it take them to learn enough to use this?

TO: **All Employees**

Sales Report To Employees

for _____
(month/year)

Product	Proj MTD $	Actual MTD $	Proj YTD $	Actual YTD $
Total Company				

Comments:

Products above projections:

Products below projections:

We were (above/below) projections for the month by _____%.

New accounts this month:

Attachments: Dollar Sales by Product, Unit Sales, Top Products/Top Customers

CHAPTER 6: PRODUCT DEVELOPMENT

Product development is the incremental process by which you make an idea into a product — and thereafter increase the product's quality and usefulness to your customer as time passes. Thus product development has to do with existing products as well as with new; indeed, most companies develop their best new products from ones they already sell. They begin developing successor products the moment they think of the original. Truly new products are rare, and no business manager waits for a brainstorm before making improvements to existing products.

However you get to the new product, the generation of new ideas is the most interesting part of product development. In many ways, it's the most creative work of the company — and as many people as reasonably can should take part.

The Sources of Innovation

This includes not only employees, but customers as well. Innovations often come from routine customer comments. The company that translates the wishes of its customers into products appealing to a broad market succeeds almost automatically.

Successful products also come from looking at what's hot in your industry, or at what your competitors do better than you do. This requires keeping tabs on your competitors; stay on the mailing lists for competitor's products and read trade journals with an eye to developments that signal new needs in your marketplace.

It's important to pursue new products even if your current lines sell well. The best kind of product development extends the interest in your products to new audiences while retaining the old. Your marketing and sales departments should welcome new

The creative work of the company

Managing innovation

products because they offer something new to talk about to customers who may have bought existing products for years. They can rekindle interest in your entire product line.

But as technology develops, it becomes more and more difficult to stay on the cutting edge in any given industry. Managers must make decisions about where their technical strengths lie, invest there and purchase other knowledge.

Historically, something like 90 percent of a company's proprietary products or technology came from in-house development and 10 percent outside. In the future, the breakdown may become 50-50, and the definition of "outside" may come to mean contract work, joint ventures, university research and consultants.

All this drives up costs, making product development not only the most creative but perhaps the riskiest function inside the organization. Managers must forecast how well new products will do and know when to make changes. They must also know when to abandon a project.

The Cutting Edge

For some companies, product development is everything, with ramifications multiplying throughout the enterprise. California-based Techwear Inc., for example, makes special lab coats and other clothing to control static electricity — a hazard in such industries as high tech electronics and medicine. Owner Kay Adams sells into a market that demands better and better fabrics, and she organizes her efforts to meet that demand.

She began the company in 1987 and has used a series of business plans "almost like a notebook" to set goals and measure her success in achieving them. Her company has been profitable since 1989. Its clients include Hewlett-Packard, IBM and Boeing. When she started out, Adams wrote down her goals, defining her market and most promising products. Now she writes a new business plan each year. Specifically, her plans include:

- A description of Techwear's industry niche;

- Financial and market objectives for the company;

- A description of Techwear's operations;

- The company's product line;

- A quick analysis of the competition;

- A description of likely customers;

- An outline of the company's marketing plan; and

- A list of company officers.

The section dealing with her product line starts with Techwear's initial product — a fabric she developed and introduced to the market — and moves through the half dozen products Techwear has developed since. Adams says this section motivates her product development efforts.

As time passes Adams has added more-detailed items to her plans — for example, marketing schedules, estimated costs, sales histories and forecasts and complete budgets.

She talks about new product development in notes to her business plans. This is "where I usually talk about ideas and looking into developing products," she says.

"Being a small business — and woman-owned — we've never been able to acquire outside financing," Adams says, echoing a common complaint. "I've been self-financing since I started out by selling my house and using my credit cards."

In her business plan for 1994, Adams focused on expanding her revenues by applying several aggressive marketing strategies, including signing up better educated and technically trained people as sales reps. The plan also identified specific territories Techwear wanted to enter, the biggest being Europe, where she thought her lab coats would sell well.

When it comes to product development, Adams often incubates ideas for a long time before she puts them in writing. But "the fact that I put them in writing makes them more clear in my mind," she says.

New ideas come to the surface

"[Also], it's kind of fun to go back to earlier plans and see how naive I was . . . holy cow, I really believed that!"

In 1993 she came up with an idea for a fabric with greatly improved static control. For the first time, she wrote product development explicitly into her business plan.

Industry types told her that the material she had in mind couldn't be developed feasibly. "I set up a prototype in the office, tested it — and it worked. I kept notes in the business plan. A patent attorney told me you need to document everything," she says. She patented the new product within three months of developing it, in January 1994, in time to generate revenue the same year.

Adams thinks the product will prove a major source of revenue in the near future. Bitten with the R&D bug, she developed a followup product and filed for a patent on that in July 1994.

Assessing Costs and Risks

New products are high risk ventures, challenging you to anticipate and minimize the risks you undertake. The chart below assesses the riskiness of a particular new product.

	EXISTING CUSTOMERS	NEW CUSTOMERS
EXISTING PRODUCTS	Lowest Risk	Some Risk
NEW PRODUCTS	Some Risk	Highest Risk

Smart managers expand their product line incrementally, moving in small steps from product to product and market to market. As they go along, they ask themselves key questions:

- Does the product come from a need you know your customers have? Or do you merely think it's a need? What's the evidence of that need?

- If specific customers want the new product more than others, can you bring them into the development process? Would they pick up some of the development costs? Would they commission the product outright?

- Will this new product fundamentally change your internal operations? If you have inventory under tight control, will this product interfere with that discipline?

- Are you counting on the quality of the product — not just value or level of service — to sell the product? If one of these three factors weighs more heavily than the others, which does?

How many competing new products are in the market already? If interest centers on a competitor's product, is there room for you?

Minimizing Risk

People in product development turn an old advertising joke on themselves: "I know half of my development money is wasted. I just don't know which half."

You minimize the loss of that money if you know that:

- You can maintain high quality with the new product;

- Customers familiar with your existing products will find the new one easy to use;

- Target customers think the product's been made just for them;

- The product adds value to your operations without adding much new cost.

Progressive companies follow the Japanese *keiretsu* model in forming partnerships with customers and vendors in developing new products. Big pharmaceutical companies such as Merck and Lilly set up deals with tiny research outfits, trading cash for marketing rights on new products. In the computer business, Microsoft and NExT hook up with big hardware makers to share R&D costs. In the automobile business, car makers

An equal footing

build partnerships with parts suppliers, giving themselves more input into product development and refinement.

Tammy Erickson, an Arthur D. Little consultant and coauthor of the book *Third Generation R&D*, worries that many companies approach product development as an afterthought. Managers prepare a business plan without considering R&D and then plug in some predetermined percentage of revenue to please their capital sources.

But if product development is a central activity within your company, give it an equal footing with marketing, operations and finance in the planning and implementation process. In this way, product development only supports the core business plan but also helps define it.

Your product development and finance people, for example, could form a partnership in budgeting for development and monitoring progress. This can prove difficult since finance people fret about the costs and risks of big R&D budgets, but it integrates the activity into everything the company does.

You can integrate product development into other functions of your business as well. For example, if you want to test design specifications with your customers, get your sales and marketing people involved in making the key contacts, and bring in those employees who will make and ship the product. If your employees find it easy to make — and if your customers find it easy to buy and use — both will work to fit the new product into their regular course of business.

Product development works best as an integrated part of corporate strategy. In this way, product development can serve multiple purposes — including integrating new technology into the company at large and suggesting new markets in which to develop business.

Monitoring New Product Development

It's tough to monitor product development. Some companies are content to lose money for decades on

R&D, in search of one huge hit. Others want to justify their R&D costs in two or three years. Both approaches can work.

In her book, Arthur Little's Erickson describes the product development approaches that three post-World War II generations of American managers have taken.

The first generation gave a pile of money to a team of bright people, locked them away in a country setting and hoped they came up with useful new ideas. R&D investments were a cost, as opposed to a strategic asset. Companies following this system tended to organize rigidly around cost centers and disciplines and rarely linked product development and business strategy.

The second generation put product development into the role of supplier. The organization told its R&D people what it needed and expected them to bring it back for sale. This generation used what Erickson calls "financial and probabilistic-driven systems" in overseeing R&D. They relied on quantitative financial language — net present value, discount and cash flow, shareholder equations, probability analysis, etc. — in communicating what happened in the black box of R&D.

The third — and current — generation built partnerships with product developers, integrating the activity into all aspects of the business and using it to think of new ways for the company to grow. This method doesn't forget budgets. Most third generation companies monitor project costs closely, and they cut off projects that don't pass muster.

The Central Question

So which method does best with R&D? Many of the major technological developments of our time came out of first generation laboratories, but that doesn't mean that modern managers should adopt that generation's practices.

Perhaps the easiest way to answer the question is to sort through all the measurements that don't measure up. Some companies judge R&D by the percentage of revenues they trace to it. This can be use-

Judging the value of R&D

ful; it certainly gives you easy benchmarks. But problems remain. Different companies define product development in different ways. Some count only pure research expenses; others include engineering staff and technological services. And different companies get technology in different ways. If you buy technology from outside suppliers, you may have no way to account for the R&D that went into the technology.

A growing number of companies use return on investment, calculating the number of years to payback, the net present value of the investment, or the internal rate of return using standard financial performance measures. But anyone who looks at the numbers with a critical eye can quickly find flaws and weaknesses.

Other benchmarks usually involve either output measures or process measures. Output measures count what R&D actually produces — the percentage of revenue generated by new products developed in the last five years, for example, or customer rating of your technological competitiveness.

A Close Focus

Process measures focus closely on management questions. How successful is your R&D section in meeting its stated objectives? How do the costs of new products compare with budget figures? How well do development projects develop and meet milestones?

However you do it, product development is so influenced by uncertainty that exact financial analysis becomes absurd. You can make the numbers say almost anything you want. You can always say market opportunity is big, and you can distort figures to make R&D budgets seem a bargain. But none of this tells you how a particular project will turn out.

Though most companies use either R&D revenues or return on investment, consultants still find it almost impossible to measure in terms of actual risk involved.

That doesn't mean you should give up on standards like percent of revenues and return on investment. It just means you shouldn't put too much emphasis on the figures that come out of that analysis. Financial ratios should be just one input into the decision process.

An Ongoing Experiment

In many ways, Karen Marchetti considers her company, Rhode Island-based Freight Control Services, one big experiment in new product development. For one thing, her company was the first of its kind in her area, so she had to sell her customers on the services she offered — essentially those of a travel agent for freight shippers. For another, she had no good idea how much demand for her services she would find.

In industry jargon, FCS provides third party logistical services to freight shippers, finding haulers for freight and arranging shipping.

"We started out using my former employer as our first client," Marchetti says. "We had access to their activity history, so we took those numbers, extrapolated figures and theorized how fast the business would grow."

Marchetti started the company in 1991. She had been a consumer of shipping at two companies and saw the opportunity to become a provider of shipping services for companies unwilling or unable to do it for themselves.

In classes offered by the SBA and a local college, she learned how to write a business plan and prepare a financial report. The program also yielded cheap consulting support — two University of Rhode Island undergraduates who helped fine tune her business plan, and a graduate student who assisted with sales and marketing research.

Her plan projected sales, costs and profits on a quarterly basis. It covered marketing costs, finances, operations, likely clients, likely suppliers, location, and geography. Marchetti found — as is often the case — that she underestimated development costs.

Benchmarks and financial ratios

In May 1991, Marchetti and her husband invested $4,000 to buy computers, a fax machine and other equipment to open FCS in a spare room at home.

Within a year, Marchetti had rented 300 square feet in a state-subsidized small-business incubator complex, at a subsidized rent. She targeted manufacturers of equipment with special shipping needs — for example, makers of machinery that's easily breakable or decalibrated. Her mission is simple: "We work to enhance the ability of clients to implement cost effective routing programs," Marchetti says.

"Cash flow, all the consultants told me from the beginning, is critical to small business," she adds.

FCS has proven "surprisingly successful" at meeting her projections, Marchetti says — on target from the start and profitable for the first time in 1993. The company ended that year with 15 regular clients and revenues of almost $100,000.

Like the seller of any new product, Marchetti found her focus changing as the company established itself. Customers buy different services than Marchetti thought they would. "Initially we thought customers would want us to do export documents," she says. "They were not as interested in subcontracting that, but they did want us to make transportation arrangements."

In arranging freight for customers, Marchetti developed proprietary software that does much of the work. Since her business is so much like a new product itself, putting together the software seemed a logical progression. In fact, she developed an entire business plan for the new product, just like the one she made for FCS.

And once her company got going, Marchetti took a course in using benchmarks and financial ratios to measure a company's development. This allows her, she says, to "find out where you are in relation to other companies in your fields" — vital knowledge when you bring out something entirely new.

Complexities and Difficulties

The essential problem is that no one knows how to quantify product development costs in simple, efficient terms. The approaches managers use run the range from sensible to silly. Some justify the costs if their peers in the company think the project good, or at least offbeat. Others strive to put a dollar sign on the time needed to bring the product to market. Others judge the amount and intensity of coverage in trade magazines or journals. Others look to the simplicity of the results, still others to the complexity of the results.

In the end, the value of research — like the value of art — lies in the eye of the beholder.

Ultimately, how much a company spends on product development may not measure how competitive the company is from a technological perspective. The company may be very competitive, but its R&D budget may not measure the effort the company puts into the activity. But if another company wanted to compete, it would have to spend a lot of money on R&D.

Or, as one consultant to the electronics industry laments: "If you only allow development based on its ability to support business objectives, aren't you hindering the freedom that allows genius?"

Basically, the right amount to spend on R&D is whatever you and your finance and product people agree you can afford. In a world in which markets change almost as quickly as technology standards, setting standard budgets based on sales or profit seems unrealistic.

This is a classic case of the difficulty people have defining opportunity costs. Maybe the best way to think of product development spending is to ask, "What do we give up if we spend the money?"

Lagging Your Own Market

A good illustration of this point: Through the 1980s, Mead Corporation's Lexis, a computer-based legal research service, dominated its field. Lexis was one of the first sophisticated and widely-used on-line

In the eye of the beholder

Paying the price for error

services, and it made a fortune for Mead, kicking more than $50 million a year up to corporate headquarters on revenues of around $400 million. In the midst of all this promise and money, Mead decided to milk the Lexis subsidiary rather than cultivate it. The company invested little money in developing or improving Lexis services.

As a result, other data providers entered the market. By the early 1990s, Lexis was only one of many legal on-line services and it lost market share fast. In 1994, Mead announced it would sell the Lexis unit, but Wall Street didn't show much enthusiasm. Financial analysts said that because Mead had relied so heavily on Lexis to bolster earnings, it would need to get several billion to make the sale worth doing. No one offered that much.

"Technology and the marketplace passed them," says a former Mead manager. "Senior management was content to remain a broker of public-domain information while competitors were developing value-added services. They paid the price."

What to Spend

In the end, no matter how important it is to long-term corporate health, product development is a discretionary item. You can survive without it, but probably not for long. You need judgment to decide how much to spend on it, and how.

One East Coast management consultant tells of a client who wanted to buy a smaller company that owned some attractive product-related technology. The consultant's job: To evaluate the worth of the technology. It wasn't easy. The consultant had to gauge the value of the technology as it would apply to various projects, estimate the uncertainty of these applications and then project the likelihood of successful integration.

"You have to treat [product development] as a portfolio of projects — some high risk, some low risk; some near-term, some long-term," says the consultant. "Adopt a portfolio approach as you would when investing your personal money. You can't guarantee you're going to make lots of money with a particular new product, so you try to balance risk. The best way to do this is to make product development an integrated process."

You can achieve this integration by distinguishing between technology development and product development and then:

- Setting aside some funding for development not directly related to business, earmarking these funds for the best ideas and biggest potential moneymakers; or

- Keeping your product development projects very focused and assigning teams assembled from various parts of the company to manage them.

Or both. The first method funds long-term, less focused projects. The second looks to the short to midterm, with careful discipline.

These efforts work consistently in many settings. For example, a Texas-based maker of plumbing products made developing new materials a priority. It gave its development team (which included sales and finance people) the freedom to think of any way in which untraditional material could be used in any plumbing products. The company ended up using plastics and other material in faucets and finishes. The product development team also found a number of applications for the company's whirlpool technology in different bath products.

This leads to the question: What happens when your new product team suggests something outside of your company's core competency?

It's a problem managers love to face. Bigger companies have a standard method for prioritizing ideas based on their ability to support business objectives and their potential risks and rewards. If an idea doesn't pass this test, it may end up sold or joint-ventured with another company.

The Bottom Line

No matter how low-tech you think your business is, you will spend a great deal of time contemplating terms like "technology" and "R&D" if you stay in

Pursue new ideas

business another ten years. This doesn't have to mean supercomputers, though. R&D means developing new products relevant to your market and refining the products you already sell.

Doing this well depends on your ability to pursue new ideas through the ordinary course of business. Small companies tend to fare best here because, being small, they remain nimble. Big or small, however, companies do poorly when turf battles erupt or factions create unwritten rules that resist change.

To get around this, managers create cross-functional teams to foster product development, calling on people from finance, marketing and operations to work together on a single new product. This can cause some confusion, but the creative upside is well worth the risk.

Customer Communication Record

This worksheet gives customer service personnel a way to document customer comments which might be useful in product development and marketing efforts.

With so much for each employee to do every day, good ideas get lost unless they have a specific means of documentation and communication. Customer feedback is like gold, and each suggestion should be reviewed by management.

You might even consider responding to these suggestions in writing. Nothing gains customer loyalty like feeling they have been heard. And customers who believe the will be heard are more likely to say something about your products. This is marketing information that many companies pay dearly to acquire.

To this end, this worksheet serves as a communications tool on several levels — and an inexpensive alternative to pricey market research.

Documenting and managing customer response is the key to using this worksheet. Give many copies to employees who talk to your customers every day and have them returned to a central location.

Encourage employees to document calls in which customers express needs for products that you don't have to offer them. They should also document who this customer is in terms of years they have been buying from you and dollar volume purchased.

Have your sales force review these comments to determine whether they have heard the same sorts of requests from their customers and potential customers.

Customer Communication Record

To: **Product Development Dept.**   **Date** _____

           Marketing Dept.   **Time** _____

From: **Customer Service Dept.**

       _____

We received a   ☐ call   ☐ letter (attached) from one of our customers.

_____

(customer name address & phone)

has been a customer for _____ years, and has purchased $ _____ from us in

total, $_____ of which has been this year. The main products they purchase from us are

_____

Their concerns were:

Comments from sales force:

However you structure your product development efforts, have the people involved look through an archive of these reports. In a basic manner, that kind of archive can tell you whether existing customers would support — or reject — a new or modified product.

Questions to ask

Is this suggestion one you've heard before?

Does the response say anything about customer response — either pro or con — to new products you're considering?

Does it say anything about new products you haven't considered?

Why aren't you producing a requested product now? There's little demand? It's too difficult to begin the process?

Who should follow up on on-going communications?

PRODUCT DEVELOPMENT PROPOSAL

This worksheet helps you consider and document the merits of product development ideas from any source: your customers, your employees, distributors, etc.

Just as with important customer feedback, unless you capture new ideas for products that come from employees, meetings, reading materials, etc., they will get lost. However, it is important to have a way to collect these ideas, and equally important to have a forum for discussion and decision making. Set up a committee to explore new product ideas, with employees from all parts of the company in attendance. If employees feel their ideas will be heard, they will be more likely to bring them to you.

Many companies also give employees a percentage of the profits from any product development their ideas have launched.

Directions

Like the Customer Communication Record, this is primarily a communications tool — though its application to product development is more clear. Hand copies of these forms to all employees and ask that they be returned to you or to a central location. Express your enthusiasm for product development and let employees know you want them to be active participants in the process.

When new ideas emerge, help employees do preliminary research by assisting them in filling out the questions asked in this worksheet, especially in regard to competition.

Product Development Proposal

Product Description:

Is this product related to products we currently sell?

Who will use the products?

Could we sell this product to current customers or is this a new market?

Estimated market potential:

How will the product be used?

Who else offers this product or one similar to it?

Product Name	Competitor Name	Price	Strengths	Weaknesses

Taking Control Series Form # 46
1994 © The Merritt Company

Is this product one we could sell easily along with other products we currently sell?

Does it have a large market potential?

Would this product be costly to produce?

Does it have direct competition? Could we produce a superior product?

How did this idea originate? From an existing product? From a gap in the market? From an unresolved customer need?

Does the origin of the idea say anything about *other* new products you might consider?

Questions to ask

PRODUCT DEVELOPMENT CHECKLIST

Overview

Even if product development is routine at your company, it is easy to realize at the last moment that some important step was missed — packaging not ordered, price discounts not set, no plan for notifying current customers, and many other common missing pieces that can undo an otherwise well-thought-out plan.

This worksheet helps you make sure you have covered all the important steps in the product development process.

Directions

Once you have decided to pursue development of a product, there are many decisions to be made and things that must be done between idea and prototype.

This checklist gives some of the many items. Chief among these: projected ship date and initial quantity. Experience is the best guide to make these decisions, but most small companies try to schedule twice the normal production time to new products and keep early batches to the smallest cost-effective unit.

While production and operations usually require the most attention during new product development, don't ignore marketing efforts. Especially if the new product moves away from or beyond traditional markets, more time and effort will have to go into sales and promotion.

Some owners and managers fall into the trap of thinking that they can sell a product *after* they've made it. Try to keep the production and marketing functions as simultaneous as you can.

This worksheet can help. Meet with your product development team regularly and review the checklist. Use it as a record of each step, and add to it items that are relevant to your company.

Product Development Checklist

Product _____

Projected Ship Date _____

Initial Quantity _____

Comments

1. Production
   - ☐ Design specifications
   - ☐ Materials required
   - ☐ Person-hours required
   - ☐ Temporary help required
   - ☐ Equipment required

2. Miscellaneous Production
   - ☐ Storage requirements
   - ☐ Other packaging

3. Other Costs
   - ☐ Licensing fees

4. Order Entry
   - ☐ Pricing discounts
   - ☐ Shipping schedule
   - ☐ Distribution

5. Marketing
   - ☐ Marketing research
   - ☐ Marketing plan
   - ☐ Pricing
   - ☐ Methods
     - ☐ Stuffers
     - ☐ Direct mail
     - ☐ Telemarketing
     - ☐ Sales reps
       - ☐ Commission schedules
   - ☐ Packaging with other products

6. General
   - ☐ Set sales goals
   - ☐ Determine costs
   - ☐ Calculate breakevens

Taking Control Series Form # 47
1994 © The Merritt Company

Have you discussed the new product and its development with all employees who will play a role in the production, marketing, or sales of this product?

Did you include their input to make this process as smooth as possible?

Did you set a realistic timetable to get everything done?

Will you have sales made as soon as the new product is ready to ship? How do booked sales change the initial quantities you'll produce?

Have internal production and operations functions gotten ahead of external sales and marketing functions? If so, what can you do to bring the two together?

PRODUCT DEVELOPMENT FORECAST

This worksheet makes a reasonable estimate of the sales of this product the first three years and makes a reasonable estimate of the costs associated with this product to determine how soon you can expect it to be profitable.

Sales are very difficult to project for any newly developed product. They are more projectable when the product is similar to one you already do, or to a market you already sell to.

Costs may also be difficult to separate out.

This is a very simple formula for looking at whether or not a new product is feasible financially. Profitability is a very important component, but there are other considerations about product development. It is essential to continue development processes not to stagnate as a company. You may also need to develop products to fill gaps for customers in order to retain other business.

Overview

The top half of the worksheet helps you estimate sales by looking at market potential and your possible share of that market.

The bottom half helps to project the costs associated with the development of the product, and the ongoing costs for materials and labor that will continue over the life of the product.

Directions

Looking at the two shaded boxes on the worksheet, is the selling price adequate to cover your costs and leave enough for an adequate profit margin?

Even if the product would be profitable soon, are the out-of-pocket development costs still prohibitive for your company?

Questions to ask

Product Development
Sales and Cost Forecast
Product _____

	Sales	This year	Next year	3rd year
A	**Total Market**			
B	**Expected % of Market**			
C	**Projected Number of Units to be Sold (A x B)**			
D	**Selling Price**			
E	**Total $ Volume Expected**			

Costs	1st year (development)	Next year (ongoing)

Cost of Goods Sold
    Materials
    Direct labor
    Research & development		

Sales & Marketing		

Overhead
    Indirect labor
    Overhead allocation		

TOTALS	A	A
Projected # of Units to be Sold {	B	B
A + B =	C	C

[1]From % on *Total Company Projections* worksheet, total overhead % at bottom of page

How do the projected sales and costs of this product compare to your other products? To your most successful product?

Do your projections seem to mirror the actual performance of other new products you've developed or your market has embraced?

If the product cost 10 percent more to develop, would you proceed? If it cost 10 percent less?

CHAPTER 7: OPERATIONS

Efficiency is the goal here, because nothing else will work if your day to day operations don't. And to work well, your operations must focus on satisfying customers and reducing costs.

If your operations people focus on one of these to the exclusion of the other, they head in the wrong direction.

Operations oversees production, quality control, inventory, shipping, maintenance, relations with vendors and suppliers, and customer service. In all of this, the goal for operations is to achieve the highest possible efficiency, making the best use of equipment and human resources — in other words, to reduce costs without damaging sales.

So operations is the natural choice to see to it that the business attains your goals for gross margin.

The Conventional Wisdom

It may surprise you to find customer service on the list of things for operations to do. The conventional wisdom puts customer service in an independent category or under sales and marketing, but in fact customer service ties in directly with quality control. Because customer service hears from customers every day, it may act as a tough but fair judge of how well your operations works. Customers don't know the details of your operations, but they know a lot about what it produces. Do things right and they don't call. Do something wrong — run out of inventory, send the wrong product, send a faulty product — and they let you know right away.

This makes it crucial to sort through customer complaints and identify what to do to correct any problem — maybe your operations department's biggest responsibility.

The simple goal

Eight performance standards

In addition, customer service ties your operations people to your customers, with whom they might otherwise have no contact. This keeps operations sensitive to the importance of the customer.

Monitoring

For obvious reasons, benchmarking is a popular tool in assessing the performance of operations. It's straightforward and, properly focused, highlights the important tasks that operations must accomplish.

But benchmarking doesn't automatically set the right goals. Would Federal Express have built its business with benchmarks tied to the performance of the U.S. Postal Service? It might have offered four day delivery to beat the Postal Service by one day. But it targeted a higher standard and gave us overnight delivery, forcing the Postal Service to measure itself against that.

The point here is that market-based benchmarks — those pegged to the performance of your competitors — serve as minimum standards, not as the be-all and end-all. They work for starters, and only if you can't come up with better standards to measure your own performance. You do better to identify best-case performance standards and aim for those, irrespective of what your competition does.

It's easy to find performance standards for operations. How well your operations people meet deadlines measures time management. Actuals versus budgets measure cost control. Random sampling measures quality control.

In setting performance standards for operations, managers look at eight items:

- Effectiveness;
- Efficiency;
- Company-wide (or total) quality;
- Productivity;
- Customer satisfaction;
- Quality of work life;

- Innovation; and
- Financial performance.

To an operations person, the fundamental objective of making money translates into production, inventory, and operational expense. Making money means keeping production high and inventory and expenses low.

A long tradition buttresses this thinking, but in fact, these days most managers with responsibility for operations spend their time doing three things — administering production, responding to crises and improving performance. Put another way, this means doing the job, putting out fires and adding new value.

Experience suggests that we spend most of our time doing the first two and not enough time doing the third. But we must do all three, and we need lots of information in order to bring it off — data detailing what happens during the production cycle, and why.

The Pay Off

The just-in-time inventory control system popularized by Japanese manufacturers shows how this information can pay off. In traditional manufacturing someone would deliver a big load of, say, car bumpers to the people on the production line who installed them — more bumpers than the workers needed for the day's output. So most sat on racks off to one side, waiting to be used.

The thinking here was that the company gained something by making one delivery of many bumpers. It did not consider the other side of the equation — namely the cost of a fat inventory. It did not measure the benefit of the single delivery of bumpers against the cost of loading up with more them than necessary.

The Japanese made that measurement, inventing just-in-time inventory control and saving themselves a good deal of money. And they did it by measuring, by gathering information about the production process and asking what it meant. American

Measure the right things

261

Overcome resistance to change

managers followed suit, though it took them a while to overcome the biases of their traditional methods. By way of example, one management consultant tells of working as a summer intern at an appliance manufacturing plant in the Midwest. Detecting some inefficiencies in the plant's painting methods, he implemented a simple quality-control standard. He gathered data on the number of appliances that passed paint inspection and plotted a defect rate chart which he posted on a bulletin board.

Workers had never seen their defect rate graphed before and showed some interest in the charts. Their defect rate dropped from about 30 percent to about five percent.

Unfortunately, the story doesn't end there. After several weeks of improved performance, an upset operations supervisor tracked down the intern and asked about the charts. The intern, expecting praise, instead got a hot lecture about the problems he had caused down the line. Because the defect rate in the painting operation had dropped so dramatically, the company would have to lay off its rework people, who had no screw-ups to fix.

He told the intern to take his charts off the bulletin board.

Clearly, information generates improvements, but not without cost. The intern's charts threatened the jobs of the rework people down the line — a bad outcome to the angry supervisor who castigated the intern.

But that doesn't mean that you choose not to act on the information you gather. Critical thinking remains a management duty. So does innovation of the sort required to overcome the resistance to change personified by the painting supervisor in this story.

The Corporate Culture

Minnesota-based Zytec Corp. stakes its fortunes on gathering and using information about the production system. The company designs and manufactures power supplies for computers, medical gear, work stations — almost anything electronic. It posts annual revenues of $100 million and employs 900 people. It came out of a management-led buyout of a Control Data Corp. subsidiary in 1984.

At the time, management committed to using *hoshin kanri,* a Japanese discipline of policy deployment that includes all elements of a company in the planning process and relies heavily on information.

John Rogers, vice president of finance, says *hoshin kanri* "doesn't really address what most people call strategic planning. We start out in the early part of any given year with a series of meetings at our senior staff and board levels to [address] major issues — things that should be included. A lot of what the outside world calls strategic planning is done ad hoc by senior staff."

In preparing for the year ahead, the company develops separate plans for technical, marketing, manufacturing, materials and corporate functions put together by interdisciplinary groups consisting 70 percent of experts in a given area and 30 percent of workers from other areas. The marketing group, for example, includes marketing staffers plus one engineer, one person from manufacturing and one from finance. Continuous improvement gets a high priority in formulating the plans, and the groups must come up with benchmarks to track improvement.

Four Objectives

Once done, the plans go to the people who implement them. Managers calculate the financial costs and benefits, and then a final version goes to the board of directors for approval. Senior managers compare the plans to coordinate their objectives. For 1994, Zytec's four objectives were to improve quality, improve the production cycle time, improve customer service, and reduce costs.

The *hoshin kanri* system comes into play in the way it implements simple goals. "In a manufacturing team [12 to 15 people working as a cell on the manufacturing floor], one person will have attended a recent long range planning meeting" on benchmarks,

Putting high value on planning

A big target

Rogers says. That person must communicate the objectives to the team — for example, to improve quality defined by faults per million — and how to go about it.

Team leaders review performance against objectives with senior staff once a month. The meetings, usually brief, present several graphs or other illustrations of the team's benchmarks. Managers say quickly which benchmarks have been met, which not. Staff then asks what resources the team needs to meet benchmarks.

Many team managers ask their entire teams to come to the meetings. Zytec has a total of 45 teams reporting monthly. So a senior manager hears 45 reports every month.

As for the payoff, Rogers offers an example. "We committed to reducing cycle time necessary to produce basic documents — accounts payable checks, payroll checks," he says. "Since 1984, we slowly reduced time to about 10 percent of '84 levels. [At that time,] something like 12 to 16 clerical people worked in accounting. Now we're substantially bigger than we were then and we have only three people there."

The system eats up the time of the people involved, but Zytec doesn't measure that cost. "It's part of our culture," Rogers says. "We don't evaluate in dollar sense; we evaluate in whether we can afford the time."

Zytec doesn't calculate the return on investment generated by the *hoshin kanri* system, either. Asked to hazard a guess, Rogers says the system might use 2,000 man hours in a year. An average salary of $30,000 would bring the tab to $30,000, plus another $5,000 in other costs. "There's no question we get $35,000 of value out of it," he says. He dismisses ROI as speculative. Instead, Rogers argues, the *hoshin kanri* system supports Zytec's vision statement in way no other system could.

That vision statement does set high standards:

> *Zytec is a company that competes on value; is market driven; provides superior quality and service; builds strong relationships with its*

customers; and provides technical excellence in its products.

Controlling Inventory

Inventory makes a big target when operations sets out to improve your company's efficiency, but it presents managers with some hard questions.

"It's good to think of inventory as a liquid force," says one New York-based consultant. "It pours around the decisions you make about your business. You can't make hard policies about how your inventory will be. The best you can do is have a few priorities and use inventory as a kind of ongoing barometer of what's going on in your business."

With service companies, "inventory" is really people available to work with clients, and the drive for efficiency leads managers to embrace nontraditional employment and compensation structures — parttime or contract workers and flexible teams operating as so-called "virtual corporations."

With manufacturing companies, some studies argue that you can reduce operating costs by more than 25 percent by managing inventory well. Things on shelves tie up cash; you spend money to make and maintain them — and then face the risk of damage or loss. Managers keep inventory as low as they can, at the risk of revenue-killing backlogs, spikes in supply costs, and production scheduling nightmares.

Losers Accumulate

Things on shelves also test the effectiveness of your marketing efforts. A quick walk through your warehouse, for example, tells you a lot. Losers accumulate, winners disappear; products that don't sell take up storage space that could go to faster movers. If your shelves groan under products that you expected to sell, ask your sales force and marketers why.

Don't stockpile losers passively — which means don't ignore your inventory mix. You can cut inventory by 50 percent and still have piles of things in

'A liquid force'

The value of good timing

your warehouse that no one wants — a permanent inventory, and expensive.

Some inventory problems have to do with the mix of products you stock, not with quantities. Retailers learn this the hard way. They balance the need to stay in stock against the need to turn inventory — a crucial measure of success in retailing. Most try to hit annual sales between 12 and 20 times inventory, which puts pressure on managers to keep only the best products in stock. A big mix of products makes their problems worse by lowering storage capacity for any single product. And retailers must remain "open to buy" — ready to purchase and stock hot items.

Managers in other businesses keep themselves open to buy by remaining flexible and market-responsive even when it means taking less of a profit than you want out of one item, so as to free up money and space for another.

Growth also makes for complications in inventory control. You can't grow faster than you can deliver product to your customers. You may have to re-plenish inventory more often or stock more units of fewer products.

It's hard to quantify the connection, but some managers see inventory numbers as a reflection of accounts payable and receivable. Government contractors, for example, wait 60 days for payment, sometimes 90 days, and their accounts receivable run a deep negative. As a result, they rarely keep inventories larger than the value of their receivables minus payables.

"You need to figure out where all the money has to go to make the business function and know what the timing has to be," says a Maryland-based consultant to government contractors. "If you're fronting a lot of money to payroll and product development, you're not [going to have much left for carrying] a big inventory. Make sure you can absorb the growth until it is paid for."

Quality Control

Operations also gets responsibility for quality control — and struggles even more than it does with inventory control.

The goal of quality control is to make sure that the things you produce work as you promise they will. Good quality control makes for efficient operations by reducing the waste that goes with shoddy workmanship; quality control prevents the production of defective items you can't sell. But there are no rules of thumb here. You can't expect to wring 25 percent out of your production costs with good quality control, as you can with good inventory control. But you can measure it — and benefit from it.

A popular accounting tool for measuring quality is first-run yield (FRY) analysis. The concept starts out simply enough: If you inspect 100 products and find that 99 meet your quality specifications, the FRY rate for that product is 99 percent.

But it gets complicated. Each step in the process of making, storing and distributing product poses a new hazard to your FRY rate. If your manufacturing path entails many processes, the total FRY becomes the multiple of the FRYs of each process. In other words, the overall FRY for a process is the FRY of step A multiplied by the FRY of step B multiplied by the FRY of step C, etc., — making a chain only as strong as its weakest link. If one process in your manufacturing chain posts a 50 percent FRY, the best FRY your company can show is 50 percent.

According to a Coopers & Lybrand study, the FRY rate averages 40 percent for companies in North America — a shocking number and a challenge to quality control.

The Answers

There are some answers. One, called operational strategic planning (OSP), essentially analyzes the facilities you use to make things and the ways in which you manage your use of those facilities. OSP seeks to bring about continuous quality improvement by studying your:

First-run yield analysis

Asking the right questions

- Process and equipment needs;

- Computer and automation methods, maintenance and specifications;

- Systems design and control;

- Facilities design;

- Assembly operations;

- Quality assurance and inspection; and,

- Production and inventory control.

OSP studies size, capacity, location, condition, specialization or focus, material handling and storage space utilization. It calculates the operating cost for each facility, compared to others within the same company or in the same industry sector.

This information in hand, OSP analyzes how management maximizes its use — or doesn't. It evaluates management information and control, design and manufacturing systems, and quality systems. It also looks at peripheral influences such as your accounting and EDP systems, since they supply management with information to measure operations performance.

Defining the Problem

The OSP review then compares the use of technical and managerial assets. It defines problems by illustrating the difference between the two by asking questions:

- Can the company's hardware and software provide accurate, timely, meaningful information in a format that management can access easily?

- Does management understand and have confidence in the information provided by the systems?

- Has management used this information to improve production performance?

- Does the organization use human resources correctly and value these resources accurately? Does it have mechanisms in place to project payroll costs (including benefits and insurance costs like workers' comp)?

- Are facilities capable of being modified to design, make and store a changing product mix?

The answers to these questions should show you how to change and improve your operations strategy. Equipment and process capacity may increase or decrease but the capability and control will usually need improvement.

Your manufacturing processes will change if you shift to a more or less vertical integration, or to more outsourcing.

Group technology and just-in-time inventory may allow new plants to be smaller, while producing the same volume as older plants.

Changes in product technology, such as replacing discrete with surface mounted components in electronic products, may allow a reduction of plant size or more production from the same plant.

Management information, control, design and manufacturing systems may need to be more sophisticated if tied to CAD/CAM and other computerized tools.

Last but not least, you may need fewer but more highly trained personnel.

OSP consultants argue that you should identify all changes and include them in a pro forma operating budget, to establish whether you can meet performance requirements. Some consultants make their livings doing this analysis, but in many cases you can run the budgets yourself. All the tools you need are in this book — many of them in Chapter 4, on financial scorekeeping.

Another quality management tool that many managers favor is called just-in-time manufacturing. This technique emphasizes the elimination of waste, defined as anything beyond the minimum equipment, materials, space and labor needed to add value to the product or service. Just-in-time manufacturing draws heavily from inventory con-

On-line quality control

trol applications and one from the next item on our list: Total Quality Management.

Total Quality Management

The inventor of Total Quality Management, W. Edwards Deming, began preaching his gospel of quality in Japan, where he went after World War II to help conduct a census. He had helped devise sampling techniques first used in the 1940 U.S. census, and in Japan Deming lectured to top business leaders on statistical quality control. He told the businessmen that Japan could dominate world markets if they stressed his definition of quality in their manufacturing operations.

Deming identified three phases of change that companies go through on the road to improved performance measurement systems:

- Tinkering with the existing measurement system (e.g. the cost accounting system);

- Cutting the "knot" between accounting and performance measurement; and

- Embracing change in strategies, actions, and measures.

Deming believed in on-line quality control rather than end-line control. To achieve it, analysts sample products during manufacture to determine the product's deviation from an accepted range of errors. As Deming saw it, any deviation is the result of one of two kinds of variables, either a special cause stemming from random events, or a common cause arising from faults in the system. Deming argued that special causes account for only 6 percent of all variations and common causes for 94 percent. (He also liked to say that bad management caused 85 percent of the quality and productivity problems in business.) In his view, most companies spend too much time trying to determine the nature of special causes rather than examining the system to find out what's behind the common causes.

Deming's analysis relies heavily on mathematics — a product of his background as a government statistician: "People who are more number-oriented are more likely to use a Deming approach," says Massachusetts management consultant Michael Galardi.

A Simple Thesis

But you don't have to be Stephen Hawking to understand Deming. He believed quality improves as variability decreases — a simple idea. To monitor variance, he advocated a statistical method of quality control. He argued that companies should strive for continuous improvement using statistical methods and analysis to maintain quality, instead of inspecting products en masse for defects once they have been manufactured.

Deming's work remained theoretical, but his many students have assembled a body of literature and consulting advice that gives the concepts a practical spin.

Growth and Quality

California-based Sunrise Medical Inc. makes wheelchairs, hospital beds and patient aids that ease the lives of the disabled and the elderly. With revenues of some $235 million a year, Sunrise doesn't count as a small company, but chairman and CEO Richard Chandler runs the company like a boot-strap operation. He cuts costs, insists on improving quality and invests heavily in product development.

Chandler founded Sunrise in 1983 with $4.5 million in seed capital raised primarily from venture capital firms. His idea came out of the fact that the growing number of elderly people and an active disabled population would increase the demand for high-quality medical products.

Sunrise had an early success with its Quickie Wheelchair division, which makes custom-built chairs designed for an individual's height, weight and color preferences. Quickie has become the country's leading maker of lightweight manual wheelchairs. The division's sales have grown some

'Define a greater purpose'

20 percent a year since 1987 and account for more than a third of Sunrise's total revenues.

Nevertheless, Chandler felt something was missing from his corporate game plan. Neither product quality nor employee motivation were as high as he wanted them to be. "People don't want to work to improve earnings per share. That doesn't turn anybody on," he told one newspaper. "You have to define a greater purpose."

That purpose came to him during a 1987 trip to Japan. After touring Toyota and Matsushita operations there, Chandler realized that Sunrise — despite its success — wasn't realizing its potential in terms of quality control.

He decided to remake Sunrise in three ways — by revamping his manufacturing operations and his research program and by improving his worker loyalty.

With respect to manufacturing, Sunrise adopted just-in-time manufacturing principles. This meant keeping a thin inventory — only material needed for producing and shipping products within 24 hours. The smaller inventories saved the company $20 million in the first four years. In addition, workers organized into self-directed teams. When a production problem arises, teams have the authority to take any actions necessary to solve it. This cut production down-time and improved employee motivation.

Product Innovation

With respect to research, Chandler decided to plow almost all profits back into product innovation. Between 1987 and 1993, research spending more than doubled to $4.21 million, or 2 percent of revenues, a year. (The company's long term goal: R&D spending of 4 percent of revenues.) The research allowed Sunrise to use advanced metals and plastics in wheelchairs, reducing chair weights almost in half. By spending $600,000 to develop an all-plastic bedside toilet chair, Sunrise created a rust-proof product 20 percent less expensive than standard metal chairs.

With respect to worker loyalty, Sunrise developed an incentive program that rewards outstanding efforts. Most of Sunrise's workers aren't highly paid; wages at one plant average less than $10 an hour. To convince workers at that level to support a quality program, the company makes its basic, company-wide goals known to all workers and celebrates achievement of specific ones.

The payoff: With improving quality and productivity numbers, Sunrise started an international expansion in the early 1990s. It made several strategic acquisitions in Europe and other markets. Its products sell in some 60 countries; international sales grew at around 30 percent annually between 1987 and 1993. The company sees 20 percent annual revenue growth through the 1990s. That would make Sunrise one of the biggest medical products makers in North America.

Deming's disciples identify ten elements of total quality management. His statistical control theories may not apply to your operations, but you can use these points as a kind of diagnostic checklist.

On a day-to-day basis, do you emphasize:

1. **Customer-orientation.** Methods, processes, and procedures are designed to meet both internal and external customer expectations.

2. **Leadership.** Top management understands the quality process and supports the strategy through both words and deeds.

3. **Full employee participation.** Everyone in the organization is provided quality training. From top to bottom, everyone has the perspective, goals, and the necessary tools and techniques for improving quality.

4. **A sensible reward system.** There is a system in place that rewards quality to ensure continuous support for the overall effort.

5. **Reduced cycle time.** There is a strong effort to reduce the cycle times, in product or service output as well as support functions, following the maxim: "If it cannot be done any better, focus on doing it faster."

'Quality is a virtue of design'

6. **Prevention, not detection.** Quality is designed into the product or service, so that errors are prevented from occurring rather than being detected and then corrected.

7. **Management by fact.** Managers use data-based feedback to measure progress; intuition and gut feeling are put on the back burner.

8. **Long-range outlook.** There is a constant monitoring of the external environment in order to answer the question: What level of quality or service must we provide to customers over the next 12 to 36 months, and how can this goal be attained?

9. **Partnership development.** The organization promotes cooperation with vendors as well as customers, thus developing a network system that helps drive up quality and hold down costs.

10. **Public responsibility.** Corporate citizenship and responsibility are fostered by sharing quality-related information with other organizations, and by working to reduce negative impacts on the community by eliminating product waste generation and product defects or recalls.

All of these characteristics apply to running a business in general. The fifth, sixth and ninth apply directly to operations.

More recently, Genichi Taguchi, another total quality consultant, has gained influence among managers with complex production and operations functions. Taguchi built his reputation as the head of research at the Electrical Communications Laboratory of Nippon Telephone and Telegraph. In 1960, he received Japan's Deming Award for his work applying quality management at a huge corporate institution.

"Quality is a virtue of design," Taguchi has written. "The robustness of products is more a function of good design than on-line control, however stringent, of manufacturing processes."

Taguchi argues that managers concentrating on the goal of zero defects have grown accustomed to viewing quality in terms of acceptable deviations from a target — rather than the effort to hit the target. The more a company deviates from targets, he contends, the bigger its losses. Taguchi quantifies this loss in a mathematical formula known as the "Quality Loss Function."

Success in the Real World

Pennsylvania-based New Standard Corp., a machine tool maker, has applied progressive management strategies to a traditional heavy-industry operation. Chairman and CEO Morton Zifferer gained notice because of his commitment to management philosophies more commonly found in high-tech, not low-tech industry.

Indeed, New Standard's plants look like industrial America from an earlier time. Its operations include almost 100 presses with rated capacities from 5 tons to 2,700 tons and specialized machines that assemble everything from high-speed impeller assemblies to parts for hedge trimmers.

But New Standard's performance would make any modern manufacturer happy. The company has reported steady growth for more than ten years. Revenues reached $30 million in 1992, up from $8.7 million in 1982. Its 300 "associates" make parts for a client list that includes Black & Decker, Caterpillar, Mack Truck and Westinghouse.

The company started out as a lawn and garden tool manufacturer in the early 1900s. Zifferer's father turned it into a repeat-order manufacturing facility. Morton Zifferer bought out his sisters in 1984 and began buying out his father in 1991.

Zifferer's business cards carry New Standard's mission statement:

> *To continuously improve our safe, secure, high integrity, team-based organization, through which we engineer and manufacture metal products that exceed our customers' expectations, assuring profitable long-term associations, while improving the quality of our lives.*

Knowing what the customer wants

New Standard's vision statement asserts that the company seeks to become "a cellular organizational structure that stimulates teamwork at all levels . . . and foster a company-wide culture that stresses continuous improvement of every process for every customer."

A Commitment

"The real opportunity is that people understand that continuous improvement is forever," Zifferer says. "We have an incredible commitment to education. We see, by 1995, all salary adjustments will be on a pay-for-skills basis."

Indeed, some company employees spend as much as 15 percent of their work day involved in some form of education, either in matters specific to their jobs or of a more general nature. "In true systems, everyone shares," Zifferer says. "You give smart people the opportunity to . . . be empowered; boil it down to a willingness to accept responsibility."

Zifferer's father taught him that being bigger wasn't better. "Being best is," he says, and he translates this into reality by practicing what he calls "agile manufacturing."

"In agile manufacturing," he says, "being able to [change operations] at the drop of a hat is what we're focusing on — getting to the point where you can anticipate what it is that your customer may not even know he wants, but you perceive it to be the delight factor in his life."

New Standard stands apart because it has accomplished so much under Zifferer's watch. In 1993, the company added four new presses to the larger of its two plants and redesigned the smaller to focus on "advance value engineering."

In 1989, Zifferer invited Ryuji Fukuda, an internationally reputed productivity expert, for a week-long seminar on improving quality. Fukuda, who has worked with Sony and Sumitomo, earned a Deming prize in the 1970s for his work on continuous quality improvement.

Zifferer boasts that New Standard worked closely on a new product development project with Black & Decker in 1993. "We worked with them from pretty crude designs through the stampings, without any blueprints," he told one local newspaper. "Other things we're looking for in the future are manufacturability and assembly but also reassembly and disassembly to replace pieces."

Zifferer says that by applying the quality control theories of people like Deming and Fukuda, his coworkers achieve high accuracy rates with traditional tools. This makes 50-year-old cutting tools capable of laser-like accuracy.

"The benchmark of quality [is] the number of defects per million," says Zifferer. "Twenty per million is very acceptable. It's a good benchmark, but once you get there, you've got to get to the next level."

The Bottom Line

Operations is the most deductive of business functions. Its objectives can be defined very clearly against predictable standards of performance and cost control.

But operations doesn't manage itself; you can't ignore operations or delegate management to junior people. On the contrary, many managers begin their efforts at overall improvement with operations because they see the most money to be saved and the greatest improvement to product quality.

For this reason, consultants count on operations advice almost as much as they count on financial advice for generating fees. But in operations as in financial matters, you can bring about a substantial improvement by using a series of basic analytic tools.

The most deductive function

UNIT OUTPUT BY PRODUCT

Overview

This worksheet gives you a method by which to monitor production output by product for each month, year to date, and on average.

You can use this worksheet to compare how many units you produce each month with how many units you sell of each product. It also allows you to see for which products you've have increased production, and for which you've decreased production (presumably due to increases or decreases in sales).

If output exceeds sales by a wide margin, you are increasing your inventory. If sales exceed output you are using up inventory, and run the risk of backorders over time.

The main benefit of doing this analysis is to post the numbers. This lets people know someone is paying attention to what they are doing. There is also the natural tendency of people to want to outdo themselves. Posting these numbers allows people to see their progress in increasing productivity.

Directions

List each product you manufacture and, at the end of each month, enter the number of units produced. Keep a running tally of total year-to-date output in the first shaded column.

Enter the average for the year in the last column.

Do this three times: once for last year, once to make projections for the current year, and once over the course of the year with actual numbers month to month.

Lastly, enter the output numbers for the prior year at the bottom of the page.

Unit Output By Product

☐ Actual last year   ☐ Projections for this year   ☐ Actual for this year

PRODUCT	1 Jan.	2 Feb.	3 Mar.	4 April	5 May	6 June	7 July	8 Aug.	9 Sept.	10 Oct.	11 Nov.	12 Dec.	Unit Output Year-to-date	Avg. Unit Output by Mo.[1]
Totals														

[1] Divide total year-to-date unit output by current month number.

Unit Output last year

Jan.	Feb.	Mar.	April	May	June	July	Aug.	Sept.	Oct.	Nov.	Dec.

Is output on the rise for all products?

Does output approximately match sales numbers?

Is output up over last year?

Are any of the trends indicative of factors that might affect production cycles in the coming year?

How do unit-output figures compare with unit-revenue figures? In other words, which are your most cost-effective products?

Questions to ask

UNITS SHIPPED

Overview

This worksheet tracks the number of products shipped each week and each month.

Another way to get a feel for sales each month is to know how many units were shipped. Even taking into consideration the variety of prices charged for different products, if units shipped are up, sales probably are too.

Units shipped is also a good gauge for determining whether to hire new production and fulfillment personnel. After using this form for a period of time, it is possible to determine how many units an average person can ship. If your totals get over this number, you may need to hire temporary help, or even hire regular help for an ongoing need.

Directions

List your products in the left-hand column. Track the number of units shipped each day for each of your products and enter the number once a week.

At the end of the month, total the columns for each week in the total shipped column. Divide this total by four or five to determine the average number of units shipped per week. Enter this number in the last column.

At the bottom of the worksheet, list units shipped in total for each month of the current year, and the prior year.

Questions to ask

Are total units shipped up over last year?

Is there a seasonality to your sales that means you have more units to be shipped at certain times of the year?

How much of your weekly and/or monthly shipments were backorders? What's your current backlog?

How do spikes in the Units Shipped figures alter your inventory control systems? Can you absorb some fluctuation? How much?

Units Shipped for _____ (month/year)

Product	Week 1	Week 2	Week 3	Week 4	Week 5	Total shipped	Average Units shipped per week
Totals							

Items shipped this year

Jan.	Feb.	Mar.	April	May	June	July	Aug.	Sept.	Oct.	Nov.	Dec.

Items shipped last year

Jan.	Feb.	Mar.	April	May	June	July	Aug.	Sept.	Oct.	Nov.	Dec.

Average Days to Ship

This worksheet helps you determine how long your customers have to wait between the time they place an order and the time the product is sent to them.

This worksheet will be most useful if you set a standard to meet. Use the average days to ship as a tracking for a service standard that you want to meet or beat.

Many companies try to ship off-the-shelf products within 24 or 48 hours of the order.

Overview

Identify your orders (usually by order number) in column one. For each order, enter the date the order was placed by the customer. In the third column, enter the date the order was actually shipped. Enter the number of days' difference between the order date and the date shipped in the last column.

At the bottom of the worksheet, take the total number of days from the shaded box at the bottom right and divide by the number of orders you have listed in the first column. This number is the number of days on average between the time the customer placed the order and the time it is shipped out to them.

Directions

Is your current average number of days to ship an acceptable number to you? What is standard in your industry?

What can your company do to decrease that number?

Does seasonality or any other external factor influence turnaround time? If so, what can you do to anticipate this?

Can you make a short turnaround time a stated goal for your company? Can you do this effectively?

Again, how do these figure affect your inventory control?

Questions to ask

Average Days To Ship

(month/year)

	Order #	Order Date	Date Shipped	Days From Order To Ship
1.				
2.				
3.				
4.				
5.				
6.				
7.				
8.				
9.				
10.				
11.				
12.				
13.				
14.				
15.				
16.				
17.				
18.				
19.				
20.				
21.				
22.				
23.				
24.				
25.				
26.				
27.				
28.				
29.				
30.				
31.				
32.				
33.				
34.				
35.				

$$\frac{\text{TOTAL days from order to ship}}{\text{TOTAL \# of orders}} = \boxed{} \quad \text{Average days to ship}$$

Taking Control Series Form # 51
1994 © The Merritt Company

At what point does the time it takes you to ship an order start to interfere with sales?

To what extent do different products require different turnaround times? Can you segregate shipping functions to handle these variations more efficiently?

RETURNS ANALYSIS

Overview

This worksheet helps you determine how many of the units you send to customers are returned to you, and why they are returned. It's a diagnostic tool.

As with many other worksheets in this section, it is important to track measures of productivity. If employees know you are paying attention to this measure, they will seek to improve the statistics themselves over time.

Directions

List your products in the far left column. Then list the total quantity returned for each product in the second column. The third column in broken into ten separate sections. Each section has a reason for return code number that is explained to the right.

Enter the total quantity returned for each reason in this section. At the bottom of the columns, enter the total numbers for reasons 1-6 and reasons 7-10.

Reasons for return numbers 1 through 6 are errors on the part of the company. Use this worksheet to track these numbers, set goals, and decrease them over time.

At the right side of the worksheet, enter the total units shipped. Calculate the percentage of shipments returned by dividing the total returns in the first shaded box by the total number of units shipped. Calculate the percentage of shipments returned for reasons 1-6 by dividing the second shaded box by the total number of units shipped.

In the area at the bottom of the worksheet, enter the number of shipments returned for reasons 1-6 for each month this year and last year.

Returns Analysis
for _____
(month/year)

Returns By Product:

Product	Total Quantity Returned	Quantity Returned By Reason*									
		1	2	3	4	5	6	7	8	9	10
Totals Returns		Total reasons 1 - 6						Total reasons 7 - 10			

*RETURN CODES
1. Product not ordered
2. Shipment received damaged
3. Wrong product received/ order entry error
4. Wrong product received/ shipping error
5. Product defective
6. Quality not as expected
7. Overstock
8. Customer changed mind
9. Exchange (old editions for new)
10. Other/don't know

TOTAL UNITS SHIPPED[1]

% of shipments returned

% of shipments returned for reasons 1 - 6

Percentage of shipments returned for reasons 1 - 6:

This year:	Jan.	Feb.	Mar.	April	May	June	July	Aug.	Sept.	Oct.	Nov.	Dec.

This month last year:	Jan.	Feb.	Mar.	April	May	June	July	Aug.	Sept.	Oct.	Nov.	Dec.

[1]From *Units Shipped* worksheet

Overall, are your returns increasing or decreasing?

Is there any meaningful link between types of product and amounts of return? Does this suggest anything for marketing or product development projects?

Are many of the returns caused by problems on your end (reasons 1 through 6), or are they mostly due to customer needs?

Do you think the number of returns could be lowered? If so, how?

BACKLOG OF ORDERS

Overview

This worksheet helps you determine whether any orders have not been shipped by the end of the week (or other period of time that you choose).

This is very important as a diagnostic monitor of production bottlenecks. A backlog occurs when an order is not shipped. This could be for a variety of reasons: The product may not be available, packaging may not be available, or shipping may be too busy to get it out.

Any items on this list should be investigated. The dollar volume column that is totalled on the bottom of the sheet will really focus your attention. Like excess inventory, backlog orders sap a company's productivity.

Knowing this report will have to be made each week will usually prompt the shipping department to get all the orders out that it can.

Directions

This worksheet should be filled in by shipping or customer service personnel every Friday. Any orders not shipped by the end of the week should be documented by order number and customer name.

Also entered should be the dollar volume of the order, and the date the order was placed. The expected ship date and comments should indicate why the order was not shipped, and when it will be.

The total dollar volume of all the orders not shipped should be entered at the bottom of the worksheet.

Questions to ask

Are there orders backlogged every week or only occasionally?

Are the reasons for backlogs usually the same?

Are these problems that can be corrected? If so, how?

Backlog of Orders

Week of _____

Order #	Customer	$ Volume of Order	Order Date	Expected Ship Date	Comments
	TOTAL				

Top 10 Vendor Log

This worksheet tracks which vendors your company spends the most money with each year and determines how much money you spend.

It is interesting to see with whom your company spends the most money each year. You may be on the list of this vendors' most important customers, and represent a relationship they would like to expand. Take advantage of this.

You can — like some aggressive managers — tell vendors that you know you spent $20,000 (or more) with them in the past year and that they might get more of your business if they're willing to negotiate on price discounts and/or terms.

It is also a good practice to look at what you are spending with any given vendor for a whole year. We often don't realize what we spend in total when we receive monthly invoices.

Taking a look at top vendors also helped my company set limits for how much we wanted to spend in particular categories.

The log also helps to spot trends where over-reliance on one vendor or source could be risky if they cannot perform.

List all of the regular vendors you send checks to each year and rank order them by top dollar volume down. Enter them by name and the product or service they provide in the first two columns. Last, enter the dollar volume you have spent with them this year. You may also want to do this exercise for the last full year and see if your spending with these vendors has gone up or down.

Top 10 Vendor Log — Critical Suppliers
(Ranked by $ Volume)

	Name	Product Or Service	$ Volume Spent With Them This Year
1.			
2.			
3.			
4.			
5.			
6.			
7.			
8.			
9.			
10.			

Taking Control Series Form # 54
1994 © The Merritt Company

Are these services that you spend so much on each year critical to the profitability of the company?

Can you bid these services out to explore whether you're getting the most value for your dollars spent?

Can you talk with any of these vendors about fee reductions for a certain dollar volume of business?

What do these expenditures suggest about weaknesses or strengths in your management structure?

INVENTORY CONTROL REPORT

Overview

This worksheet helps you determine your total inventory over a set time period and where your inventory is inadequate to meet sales needs.

This is another very important indicator of production bottlenecks.

Any items listed at the bottom of the page should be questioned. Asking the right questions at this stage could prevent these products from showing up on the backlog list later.

Directions

Enter the total inventory numbers from the year at a glance financial analysis worksheet for each month this year and last year.

In the section below, list all products with less that two months' inventory at current sales levels, quantity currently on hand, and when restocking is expected.

This worksheet is an essential step in any move toward a just-in-time inventory management system.

Questions to ask

Is total inventory going up or down?

Does inventory fluctuate in a cyclical or seasonal pattern? If so, can you use these patterns to manage inventory in the future?

Does this increase or decrease fit with your cash management strategies?

Will your restocking dates allow you to replenish your inventory supply before you run out of product?

What do inventory fluctuations suggest about your market sector? Your customers? Your internal operations?

Inventory Control Report
for _____
(month/year)

Total Inventory

This month:

Jan.	Feb.	Mar.	April	May	June	July	Aug.	Sept.	Oct.	Nov.	Dec.

This month last year:

Jan.	Feb.	Mar.	April	May	June	July	Aug.	Sept.	Oct.	Nov.	Dec.

Inventory At Low Level:

List below any items with under two months inventory on hand.

Product Description	Quantity Currently On hand	Expected Restock Date

CUSTOMER SERVICE KEY INDICATORS

Overview

This worksheet helps you monitor the workload and productivity of the customer service representatives and the department as a whole. It's a diagnostic tool.

Keeping the pulse of activity in customer service can be a general indication of how well the company is running. This worksheet and any other measurements of customer satisfaction are key to a general determination of operational efficiency. The worksheet can be used to track the productivity of the individuals who answer your telephones.

Posting these measurements will give rise to the natural competition between individuals, especially for sales dollars.

Directions

List each customer service representative by name and, if your telephone equipment and computer equipment will allow, enter the number of calls each has answered the percentage of time on the phone, the percentage of time they are not available to take calls, and the dollar volume of sales per sales rep.

At the bottom of the worksheet, tally the number of calls in each category over the past two years by month.

The bottom half of this worksheet is a good indicator for sales. It seems the more calls received, the higher the sales dollars for the month. If complaint calls have increased, it may be a measure of problems in shipping or in the quality of the product.

Customer Service Key Indicators
for _____
(month/year)

Name _____	This mo.	YTD
Calls answered	_____	_____
% time on phone	_____	
% time not available	_____	_____
$ Sales per terminal	_____	_____

Name _____	This mo.	YTD
Calls answered	_____	_____
% time on phone	_____	
% time not available	_____	_____
$ Sales per terminal	_____	_____

Name _____	This mo.	YTD
Calls answered	_____	_____
% time on phone	_____	
% time not available	_____	_____
$ Sales per terminal	_____	_____

Name _____	This mo.	YTD
Calls answered	_____	_____
% time on phone	_____	
% time not available	_____	_____
$ Sales per terminal	_____	_____

TOTALS

Last Year

	Jan.	Feb.	Mar.	April	May	June	July	Aug.	Sept.	Oct.	Nov.	Dec.
Calls received												
Calls answered												
Calls abandoned %												
Average talk time												
Calls categorized: Orders												
Inquiries												
Complaints												

This Year

	Jan.	Feb.	Mar.	April	May	June	July	Aug.	Sept.	Oct.	Nov.	Dec.
Calls received												
Calls answered												
Calls abandoned %												
Average talk time												
Calls categorized: Orders												
Inquiries												
Complaints												

Taking Control Series Form # 56
1994 © The Merritt Company

Are numbers of calls answered going up or down?

Are order calls going up faster than the number of calls in general?

Are complaint calls going up?

How do the numbers of calls you receive relate to the various products you make or market sectors you serve?

How do per-unit revenue or profitability numbers relate to customer service contacts?

Can you find ways to reward super performers in terms of numbers of calls taken and sales volume?

Questions to ask

HUMAN RESOURCE KEY INDICATORS

This worksheet allows you to gauge the morale, productivity and efficiency of the workforce.

Generally absenteeism will go up when employees are taking vacations in the summer. Watch for generally higher absenteeism within departments as a possible trend of discontentment.

If you have staffed correctly, temporary labor and overtime should be zero most months. An increase two months in a row could indicate a more regular need that should be filled. Because overtime pay is higher than regular pay, some employees will regularly find reasons to work extra hours. All overtime requests should be approved in advance to keep this extra premium to a minimum.

Tracking trends and asking the right questions should let employees know that you are watching this expense carefully.

I also track the number of suggestions in the suggestion box as a general indicator of morale problems. If you see a sudden increase, consider it a sign for concern and take steps such as an employee survey to determine the reasons.

Overview

List for each department the number of days missed due to the variety of reasons listed, and get the average days missed per employee by dividing the total days missed by the number of employees.

Also determine the amount of money spent on overtime and temporary help by entering the number of hours worked and multiplying by the rate per hour.

If you use a suggestion box, tally the number of suggestions and attach them to this worksheet.

Directions

Human Resource Key Indicators

for _____
(month/year)

Absenteeism (# of days missed this month):

Department	Vacation	Sick Leave	Personal Leave	Total	# of Employees	Average/ Employee

Overtime:

Department	# of Hours	Overtime Premium	$	Total $

Temporary Labor:

Department	# of Hours	$ Rate/Hour	Total $

Attached: ☐ **number of suggestions from Suggestion Box (attached)**

Are employees in certain departments taking more time off than those in others? Does this suggest anything about the type of work or management that goes on in different departments?

Are some departments making up for lost time with overtime or temporary help?

Can efficiency be increased to reduce the need for overtime or temporary labor?

Are there specific, meaningful connections between fluctuations in human resources indicators and spikes in inventory or order backlogs? If so, what can you to smooth out these spikes?

CONCLUSION: WINNING THE GAME

My company had the good fortune to be so profitable and cash rich in its formative years that there'd been little need to project or monitor sales or expenses, cash or profit. The downside of this: Very little had in fact been done to monitor performance. It was hard to tell how well we were doing at any given time — or would do in the future.

An entrepreneur who starts a company often has such an instinctive feeling about the business that he feels he can guess what sales will be, and spends money according to how profitable the company has been in preceding months.

By the time I began running the company, this was no longer the case. It didn't occur to me to call the CPA or look at the financials. The first thing I did was to ask our accounting department for a list of vendors to whom we wrote checks and a list of those checks. Because the checks were listed by payee, with no notation of what was being paid for, it still didn't answer my questions, so we used this list to get back to the record of the invoice that was being paid.

Much to the horror of the orderly accounting department, three of us took boxes and boxes of old invoices from our warehouse to my office to do a manual audit.

Company invoices are much like the bills I paid at home: I knew we paid rent, utilities, insurance and that we paid people. I also knew that we paid for the product we produced and its marketing. Then, of course, there were many other items like the outside professionals, computers, and miscellaneous items like office supplies.

Over several weeks, we sorted these invoices from the just-ended fiscal year into categories that

Monitor performance

Creating a goal

seemed to make sense and covered all the types of invoices we found.

In questioning people about what each individual invoice pertained to, we found — to our amazement — that many bills had been paid for services we no longer received. This seemed particularly true for maintenance contracts on equipment we had sold years before. Once the accounting department had been told to expect a particular bill each month, they continued to pay it without question. Many bills are addressed to accounts payable, and paid without anyone else ever seeing them. We cut about $77,000 in expenses simply by questioning old invoices.

I came to the position of CEO with an advantage in building a game plan: I thought all the other employees were just like me — smart, but uninformed. Ready to learn, but with no available teachers. For years we had all second guessed management decisions; now we were calling on ourselves to make the important decisions.

After I had been CEO for two years, the founder of the company died, leaving us without a plan for a change in ownership. The company was already 40 percent employee owned, and we were decided together to take it to 100 percent.

Creating a goal like this one creates unbeatable motivation. Suddenly, our definition of winning was more similar to an athletic game — there was a real dollar number we had to meet or beat to win. This was the genesis of the game plans I've used. They gave people real reasons to hold tight on expenses, and develop new products — reasons that people could get excited about for personal reasons. Every person working at the company had a reason to step up to the plate.

An amazing thing happens when an objective becomes as clear as this. People begin to act in concert — truly, like a team. Every action becomes focused on achieving the objective.

We decided to set up a group of committees that would meet weekly and make sure the plans we made were being implemented. The two major committees we set up monitored profitability (mostly from the revenue side) and expenses. Reporting to these committees were other subcommittees devoted to new products, customer service, strategic alliances, and other business functions. I asked for volunteers to serve on the major committees, and made sure that members from each department were present.

Many of the worksheets in this book are used by our committees to monitor performance and progress toward our goal of 100 percent employee-ownership. The committees and worksheets are forms of self-measurement. They allow employees to be responsible for deciding what work needs to be done, and then for measuring what they do.

We also made extensive use of outside experts. As a group, we call in consultants from all sorts of disciplines — marketing, corporate function, employee benefits, compensation and general finance.

Most owners and managers who've had bad experiences with consultants get bogged down in billable hours before any constructive work gets done. We find that analyzing our performance so closely allows to use consultants well. We know which questions need to be answered — and we can ask them in a focused and knowledgeable manner. We don't waste anyone's time — including our own.

Most of the consultants we use become our biggest fans. Because they appreciate the challenges we face and the serious way we do business, they'll usually work harder for us than they do for other clients.

So far, we're winning at the game. We've made the first payment due in a three year plan to buy the company. By 1996, we plan to be 100 percent employee-owned . . . and facing a new set of management challenges.

A caveat: If you choose the path of inclusive management, you will be doing something for which little precedent exists. You will find little yet in the management literature to support you or guide you in the difficulties you will encounter. Despite a host

Empowerment means sharing tools

of experts who talk about "empowerment," few practical models exist.

Empowerment should mean imparting the wisdom and sharing the tools with which to do a job successfully. And in doing so, you may be giving them more responsibility than they want. I've asked myself the following questions:

Are you not taking responsibility for managing the company — and isn't that your job, not theirs?

Are you passing the buck to your employees for decision-making? Is this something like a fundamental problem with democracy—are less capable, informed, and trained people making decisions?

Is decision-making too decentralized?

Are you making peoples' lives more complicated? Are you creating chaos instead of clarity?

I hope the answer to these questions is no. Struggling with these issues and allowing employees to struggle with their own problems is the only answer I am satisfied with. I want to create an environment with minimal rules, lots of open communication and sharing of information, and high quality thinking.

Celebrate your successes as a group and jointly take responsibility for your defeats. Watch the scoreboard and give your people reason to watch, too. Keep your operations simple and strong. Do this, and you'll win with a properly executed game plan.

APPENDIX ONE:
CHOOSING AND USING CONSULTANTS

One of the aims of this book has been to give owners and managers the tools to be their own consultants — and to avoid one of the major expenses that many small companies carry.

Wisconsin-based Mid-States Aluminum Corp. had increased its sales by 20 percent per year between 1984 and the early 1990s. But the bottom line was not expanding at anywhere near that rate.

CEO Joe Colwin spent months walking around his 200-employee, 30-year-old company looking at the way things were being done. He knew something was stunting profits, but he couldn't figure what exactly that something was.

So he contacted the nearby office of a major, national management consulting firm and asked them to come in and take a look at the company.

The results were stunning. The consultants had a third of Colwin's employees in administration, sales, marketing, engineering, production, purchasing and human resources keep track of what they did each day. They found that of 160,000 hours the 78 people spent on the job, only 22 percent added any value to the customer. The rest was mostly redundant, repetitive work that ate up both time and dollars.

The analysis found that cycle time for generating quotes, entering orders, retooling, producing and finally shipping at Mid-States was about 73 days. Some 81 percent of that time was "wait time" in which the order was in limbo. Overall, the consultants found that nearly $2 million of annual costs were not adding value to the Mid-States customers.

As a result, Colwin set up an information system to qualify quotes so that efforts are focused on those quotes with a higher probability of becoming orders. He established a system for reviewing lost quotes to develop more effective targeting criteria. Finally, he reorganized the sales unit, delegating the administrative task of generating estimates and quotes to clerical employees so the sales force could spend more time selling.

In general, Colwin used the consultants' analysis to choose what information he shared with employees. After their analysis was completed, he limited their role to occasional advisory meetings. Once the problem with down-time was articulated, the company began to heal itself. Within a few months, Mid-States employees had devised ways to eliminate 5,000 hours of non-value-added work.

Many owners and managers are suspicious of consultants; they distrust freelance experts who charge big hourly rates but make little long-term commitment. Sometimes, they resent any outsider criticizing their companies — no matter how much they know, intellectually, that they need help.

However, the fact remains that some managers at some companies need to hire experience or expertise from the outside. Reasons you might need some outside help include:

- you need a high or specific level of expertise that goes beyond what your company could afford to pay to an employee;

- your needs, generated by growth or external market forces, are only temporary;

- problems have become so acute that they require immediate response;

- problems are of such a broad institutional nature that they defy internal response.

How do you know you're in this kind of position? You're calling the bank every day — nervous to hear your account balance because you can't get straight information from your accounting department. Traditional marketing campaigns that have worked for years take a sudden dive in performance. Production bottlenecks you never saw before flare up and won't go away.

Unfortunately, identifying a problem isn't the same as fixing it. That's where outside consultants — used well — come in. But you have to look past short-term tensions to long-term goals. You have to be willing to share relevant information freely and cooperate openly. This doesn't mean handing over the keys to your kingdom, but it does mean you have to do some preliminary work and expand your concepts of trust and comfort to include some outsiders.

Done well, these efforts will return many times their original investment. They'll get you past sticky problems and lead you into productive relationships with the best consultants in their fields.

Consultants have a bad reputation among some owners and managers for two basic reasons: first, because there are many bad ones; second, because many clients use consultants badly.

In the 1980s, the number of business consultants — especially financial consultants — grew substantially. Exact numbers are hard to find, but conventional wisdom (culled from studies by groups such as Grant Thorton & Associates, Hewitt & Associates, the Rand Corporation and Korn/Ferry International) pegs the business consulting market at around $4 billion. There are a lot of business experts happy to work with small, growing companies. However, as a potential buyer, you should beware. Not every consultant is a McKinsey Co. or Tom Peters.

Erratic use makes problems of erratic quality worse. Often, the owners and managers who complain most about consultants use them in the most ill-advised ways. Horror stories usually include some variation on this theme:

A manager knows someone or meets someone whose ideas and expertise impress people (primarily, the manager himself or herself). The someone may be a consultant, or may become available because of a career change. The manager likes the someone's ideas or energy or charisma — but doesn't have a suitable job available. So, the manager hires the someone as a consultant on some non-specific basis like "improving performance."

A scenario like this is destined for trouble. If you want people with good ideas and energy and charisma around you, hire them as employees. Save consultants for more specific goals.

Most consultants market their services by word-of-mouth. As a result, when owners or managers think they need someone, they usually do best to ask friends or peers for names. But recommendations don't assure success. The key to success lies in interviewing consultants well.

The following questions—and answer guidelines—can help you interview prospective consultants and choose the right one for a given time and circumstance.

1) Most consultants focus on two areas: cutting costs and raising revenues. What do you see as the relationship between the two functions? Which do you do better?

Cost-cutting is the consultant's usual expertise. It's what most companies need. A 1994 Grant Thorton survey of 250 top executives found that 84 percent of those who'd recently restructured their companies did so to reduce costs.

Most of these hired outside consultants to take an objective look at organizational charts, value-adding processes and competitive environments. "We spend a lot of time talking to a company's customers, so we understand what they like and don't like," one Ernst & Young consultant says. "What does the customer value? Is it time? Is it quality? We define that."

What this means is that a company can cut jobs and still not touch on one non-value-added activity or add value to the customer.

2) What was your professional experience before you became a consultant?

Ultimately, you should want any consultant you use to have a strong bottom-line sensibility. You want this person—or team—to focus on the things that will add the greatest amount of value to your company in the shortest amount of time. This kind of thinking doesn't come naturally to many people. It usually demands two kinds of experience: as a chief executive officer or as a corporate turnaround specialist. A consultant who has this kind of experience has dealt with strict cost controls, high-pressure scrutiny and the need for quick results. These are the same traits you should look for in anyone giving you expert advice.

Though it may seem counter-intuitive, you might look for bankruptcy and similar work-out experience from a consultant. The urgency learned in that environment applies well to the urgencies of daily business life.

3) How many professionals work with you or at your firm?

Business consultants fall essentially into two categories: Solo-practitioners and team players. The differences between the two usually involve the type of work they take. Most of the time, the soloists deal with less-specific, strategic or vision-related issues; the teams get into more tightly-focused number crunching. Less-specific functions tend to take less time (sometimes as little as one day); the more-specific take more.

One of these functions isn't better or worse than the other. The trap to beware: The marketing soloist who claims he or she can also review all of your accounting. The exercises in this book will help you make your financials easier to understand, but don't expect one consultant to fix all your problems.

4) Will you sign a letter of confidentiality? Will you refrain from working for our competitors?

Ask all consultants to sign a letter of confidentiality. Some owners and managers assume that short-term, strategic consultants pose less of a threat to proprietary interests than the number-crunchers. Don't make that assumption. You and your staff should feel free to discuss any business subject with your consultant and trust his or her discretion. If you feel uncomfortable, you won't discuss things candidly. Your risk in these cases isn't usually that the consultant will knowingly steal proprietary information or material. Most are professional enough — and work in small enough markets — that reputations matter. More often, the risk involves a consultant unwittingly mentioning something. If he or she has signed a confidentiality letter, he or she will be more likely to think twice.

5) Who are some of your other clients? Who are some people and companies with whom you've worked before? Can I call them to ask about your work?

Don't be wowed by big-shot former clients. At big companies, consultants are hired in teams to tackle extremely specific projects. Just because the guy in the $800 suit claims Chrysler as a former client doesn't mean he knows Lee Iacocca on a first-name basis. In fact, it's better if the consultant has worked with companies closer to your size and shape. They'll more likely understand your needs.

6) With how many clients do you work at one time? Do you have enough time to devote to our company to accomplish our goals? Will you return phone calls on the same day?

Asking other or former clients about the consultant's responsiveness and attentiveness can be helpful. As can more pointed questions of the consultant.

These questions all focus on the same point: How much attention can the consultant afford to spend on your needs? The number of clients a consultant can serve well varies with the kind of service provided and client involved. But some general rules apply: You want to have same-day response to questions or problems. If you're undertaking a major restructuring, you probably don't want your consultant working with more than two or three other clients.

A caveat: Some owners and managers who've had bad experiences with overly invasive (and expensive) consultants warn that you shouldn't be the *only* client a consultant has.

7) Will you teach us to do this work for ourselves and become self-sufficient? How long will this take?

One common trap in using a consultant is becoming dependent on him or her. From the consultant's perspective, this may simply be good business — assuring future work for himself, herself or themselves. From your perspective, it may be little better than the status you had before you had the consultant come in.

By making training part of the consultant's job, you can limit the chances of a prolonged engagement. Establish a schedule within which the consultant can accomplish his or her goals. Assign a staff person to work closely in this process — and learn everything he or she can.

8) Have you written anything — published or not — that deals with issues like the ones this company faces?

Consultants love to write about their experiences and their theories. Sometimes this can be pretty rough reading, but it will usually help you understand how the consultant sees markets and business factors that may affect you.

Also, management or technical literature can be a good place to look for consultants. While the latest management guru writing for the Harvard Business Review may be beyond your needs and means, you might be able to find useful experts in trade or regional newspapers and journals.

9) How do you charge for services? Do your fees include travel time and other miscellaneous charges or are those billed separately?

There's no set standard for paying consultants: Some work on a straight-fee basis, others work for a fee plus performance bonus, a few work on a contingency basis — tied to sales increases or cost reductions.

As with paying any outside contractor, your concerns should be assuring a high quality of work and containing costs within a predetermined budget.

With consultants, focusing their use as specifically as possible will help accomplish both of these ends.

Also, make it clear from the beginning what incidental expenses you're willing to pay and how you'll pay them. Consultants who've worked at or for large corporations may be used to expense accounts that you aren't. Be very clear about how much you're willing to spend on the whole project or series of projects. Insist that the consultant warn you — in writing — if the project won't be completed on time and within budget.

10) What kind of documentation will you give us when the project is completed? Who will own that documentation?Keeping a paper trail of the work a consultant does for you accomplishes several ends — all of them good.

First, if the consultation has worked well, this will usually give you some forms and tools that you can use to improve some part of your performance.

Second, it allows you to keep a record of the analyses made of your company and the responses you've taken. This kind of "scrap book" can be a big help when dealing with future problems or other consultants.

Third, it makes clear what the consultant did — and didn't do — while working for you. If any disputes should emerge over payment or ownership or confidentiality, you'll have some support.

In general, all work (including spreadsheets, computer programs, mechanical devices or literature) a consultant does for you is your property. Sometimes — especially in the cases of devices and literature — this becomes an issue. Make it clear from the beginning that you want to own everything that comes from the consultation.

Of course, you should talk to as many consultants as you can before hiring one. Even if you have one person or firm in mind, interview at least a few others as a sort of due diligence. You'll probably find that each interview helps you focus on the issues you're hiring a consult to help resolve.

Do the interviews in a comfortable place. In some cases, this might mean a neutral location and setting — over lunch or in some kind of recreational setting. Being away from the office sometimes helps people think about problems in more objective terms.

When you've found a consultant that seems promising, use the interview to test his or her response to one or two of the real problems you're facing. You don't have to recreate every detail of your problem; boil it down to its essential elements and pose it as a sample of the kind of work you're anticipating.

This kind of question works on two levels. First, it gives you a sense of how the consultant works in a short amount of time with rudimentary information. Second, it lets you know what kind of response the consultant gives. You can judge these things on a personal level as well as a professional. Ask yourself if this is the kind of person with whom you'd feel comfortable working. Does she respond quickly enough? Does he think carefully enough? Is she too reserved? Is he too extreme?

Working intensely with an outside critic and analyst of your company will require a certain level of personal affinity — at least some similarity in style. While you don't have to (and probably shouldn't) have a personal relationship with a consultant, you shouldn't underestimate the importance of professional compatibility.

A good consultant will relate to your company and your goals and make immediate contributions. Sometimes the best work a consultant does comes when he or she is new to your company.

Interviewing consultants carefully also helps you avoid wasting their time — and your own — later on. Using a consultant effectively and well depends to a significant degree on how you set the relationship up initially. The following steps explain this process more succinctly.

1) Do your homework before the consultant comes in.

Too many owners and managers hire a consultant and then stop thinking. They present a list of general problems and expect the expert to conjure dramatic results. This approach almost always ends in frustration and many, many billable hours.

Instead, you have to take the initiative. Discuss your needs, problems and parameters in candid terms from the start. Set a budget or schedule for each project a consultant tackles up front. Save your skepticism (or your staff's) for the interview process; once you've chosen a consultant, give him or her everything you've got.

Know what you need and what the relevant information would say.

One of the biggest cost-drivers in hiring outside expertise is bringing people up to date on your company's operations. It's a cost-driver that you can control, though. But keep the consultant away from data-gathering and other basic reporting functions; keep them focused on analysis.

You can tabulate numbers yourself, you've hired the expert to help you move forward from there.

If you're able to keep records over even a short period of time, you can hand the consultant your paper trail and ask him or her to read the performance numbers directly. The worksheets in this book are designed to serve that purpose.

Another point to consider: Many consultants have a steep sort of "half life" in regard to enthusiasm for a project. In other words, their best thoughts and greatest creativity come early in their relationships with clients. Being prepared from the start allows you to take full advantage of short attention spans.

2) When you hire consultants, keep in mind that their most important skill should be critical analysis and problem solving. Give them specific goals. Don't just say you have problems.

In short, know what you need. A temporary executive? An outside thinker to help jump-start your ideas? An arbitrator for internal disputes?

To the extent you use consultants as managers, try to limit them to so-called "bridge management" functions. Bridge management simply means an outside consultant will oversee a business function between permanent managers or during periods of particular turmoil.

Reasons that owners and managers hire bridge managers:

- handling excess workloads caused by projects or increased business;

- bridging gaps when down-sizing takes place;

- testing the need for a position or the person being considered for hire; or

- handling specific short-term tasks that call for experience and objectivity.

Give bridge managers clear instructions and schedules for the work they will do.

3) Give short deadlines, even a series of these, instead of open-ended ones. Consultants may serve operational functions for set periods of time but they shouldn't manage — in the broad sense of that word.

Like any outside contractor or vendor, consultant services are a commodity — and consultants want to sell as much of this commodity over as long a time as they can. That's their understandable inclination as business people. However, it's your understandable inclination as an owner or manager to minimize the bills you pay them.

They may be right to say there aren't quick fixes to serious problems. But don't let that lead to open-ended engagements. Most consultants agree that restructuring involves two phases: a design phase, in which new ways of doing work are fashioned; and an implementation phase, in which the new ways of doing work actually are put in place. Have the consultant schedule these phases.

This helps set up an exit strategy for the consultant, which is an important cost control tool. The consultant sees the project as a limited engagement, rather than an open-ended thing.

4) Keep the hierarchy clear. Have the consultant report to the fewest people possible — one, if that can be arranged.

As we've discussed elsewhere, the best way to do this is to keep the agenda simple and clear. When you hire a consultant, write up a short memo that tells the relevant people in your company who this person is and why you've hired him or her. Also, specify where and how they fit in the organizational chart. Avoid confusion of authority and responsibility.

One woman, who worked as a bridge manager for a North Carolina bank in the early 1990s, found that two factors ensured success. First, the senior manager made sure that everyone effected was informed of her arrival and her background. This gave her instant credibility. Second, the terms of her appointment were clearly spelled out. "I had a contract, and I treated the job as if it were my own, but I clearly knew that this was only for a certain period," she says.

5) Keep the consultant focused on value-adding functions.

This is another cost-control tool. Many owners and managers refuse to hire a consultant to work on anything that a customer wouldn't pay for himself or herself. Customers will usually pay for value they receive — rather than reward companies for being efficient in some sort of abstract sense. The consultant's image of operational perfection may sound great in a management journal, but do little in the marketplace.

For example, consultants often focus on staffing and personnel issues as a means of increasing efficiency. But that's not always the best approach to take. If your product costs $10 to produce with labor costs of $1 dollar and you cut out half the labor cost (a major achievement), you've still only reduced your cost by five percent. If the retail price of your product is $20, you've only cut 2.5 percent. The consultant will boast he or she has cut labor costs in half — but the retail customer won't be so impressed.

Ultimately, processes that don't add value to the customer erode a company's competitiveness.

6) Set regular times (on a weekly or monthly basis) when the consultant will review conclusions, answer questions and challenge you on better ways to run your business. But make sure these are *working* meetings. Avoid meetings that turn into administrative updates.

By meeting with the consultant on a regular basis, you can compartmentalize — and better control — the amount of time you spend with him or her. It also forces the consultant to be succinct and not draw on too much of your time. In this context, you can expect more from a consultant than from an employee. Their attention should focus squarely on problems you're paying them to consider, not on operational details.

This approach may not be practical in the midst of an intense project, but it will be a good way to use the consultant before and after that intensity. And not all consulting relationships have to be intense, at any point.

7) Don't tolerate jargon or vague or non-specific conclusions. And don't be afraid to ask so-called "dumb" questions.

Because consulting is a business that relies on a constant stream of new ideas, some consultants become immersed in trendy terms. For example, phrases like "business process innovation," "business process reassessment," "core process redesign" and "business process reengineering" all mean the same thing — restructuring your company. Some financial and management consultants revel in technical language and jargon. It's an easy way of making themselves appear better informed and qualified than each other — and potential clients. This can present a bewildering array of information and advice. Wise people from Benjamin Franklin to Stephen Hawking have said that true intelligence is the ability to explain complicated concepts in simple terms.

Remember that consultants you hire work for you. They should answer the questions you ask in language you prefer. Insist that they do.

Specific Applications

Here are some more detailed uses owners and managers often find for consultants:

- running focus groups drawn from your customers

- producing or reviewing long-term strategic plans

- analyzing divestitures, mergers or acquisitions

- changing the methods by which performance is rewarded

- helping you use technology more effectively

- interviewing your employees to help you discover how they feel about the direction of the company

- assessing the effectiveness of your staff and analyze your workforce

- proposing new staffing mixes, which bring together individuals who contribute to a particular solution

- changing job descriptions to lower costs, reduce waste and improve the quality of their products and services

- speaking to your board of directors or lenders to increase the management credibility. (In good situations, this kind of effort won't be needed. But not all situations are good. Still, a better solution: Use the worksheets in this book to track your performance and share the results with your board.)

- finding investors or other sources of equity funding.

When you keep consultants disciplined and focused, you can use them to great advantage.

APPENDIX TWO: LIST OF RESOURCES

A wide range of books, articles, lectures and computer software programs have influenced my thinking on owning and managing a company. I've put together a bibliography of the resources that have been most useful to me in making the argument that owners and managers can take more effective control of their companies.

BOOKS AND ARTICLES

Setting Direction

Rhonda M. Abrams, *The Successful Business Plan: Secrets and Strategies*. California: Oasis Press, 1992.

Warren Bennis, *An Invented Life: Meditations on Leadership & Change*. Chicago: Addison-Wesley, 1993.

Warren Bennis, *On Becoming a Leader*. Chicago: Addison-Wesley, 1989.

Anita Brattina, "The Diary of a Small-Company Owner." *Inc.*, May 1993 and June 1993.

Stephen Covey, Roger Merrill, Rebecca Merrill, *First Things First: A Principle-Centered Approach to Time & Life Management*. New York: Simon & Shuster, 1994.

Philip Crosby, *Leading: The Art of Becoming an Executive*. New York: McGraw-Hill Books, 1990.

Max DePree, *Leadership Jazz*. New York: Currency/Doubleday, 1993.

Joseph Juran, *Juran on Planning for Quality*. New York: The Free Press, 1987.

Robert Kaplan, David Norton, "Putting the Balanced Scorecard to Work." Harvard Business Review, September-October 1993.

John Kerr, "The Best Small Companies to Work for in America." *Inc.*, July 1993.

Michael E. McGill and John W. Slocum, Jr., "Unlearning the Organization," *Organizational Dynamics*, Fall 1993.

Burt Nanus, *Visionary Leadership: Creating a Compelling Sense of Direction for Your Organization*. San Francisco: Jossey-Bass Publishing, 1992.

Lee Tom Perry, Randall G. Stott, and W. Norman Smallwood, *Real-Time Strategy*. New York: John Wiley, 1993.

Tom Peters, *Thriving on Chaos*. New York: Alfred A. Knopf, 1987.

Tom Peters, *Liberation Management*. New York: Alfred A. Knopf, 1992.

Tom Peters, *The Tom Peters Seminar*. New York: Vintage Books, 1994.

Neil Snyder, James Dowd, Dianne Houghton, *Vision, Values & Courage: Leadership for Quality Management*. New York: Macmillan, 1993.

Jack Stack, *The Great Game of Business*. New York: Currency/Doubleday, 1993.

Kevin Tourangeau, *Strategy Management: How to Plan, Execute & Control Strategic Plans for Your Business*. New York: McGraw-Hill Books, 1981.

Setting Budgets

Julie Brooks and Barry Stevens, *How to Write a Successful Business Plan*. New York: American Management Association, 1992.

John Day, *Small Business in Tough Times: How to Survive & Prosper*. New York: Pfeiffer & Co., 1993.

David E. Gumpert, *How to Really Create a Successful Business Plan*. Boston: Inc. Publishing, 1992.

Richard M. Hodgetts and Donald F. Kuratko, *Effective Small Business Management*. Fort Worth, Texas: Dryden Press, 1990.

Arthur H. Kuriloff, John M. Hemphill Jr. and Douglas Cloud, *How to Start Your Own Business...And Succeed.* New York: McGraw-Hill Books, 1993.

Mike McKeever, *How to Write a Business Plan* (4th. edition). Berkeley, California: Nolo Press, 1993.

Barry Miller, Donald Miller, *How to Interpret Finacial Statements for Better Business Decisions.* New York: AMACON, 1991.

Randolph Pohlman, *Understanding the Bottom Line: Finance for Non-Financial Managers & Supervisors.* New York: National Press Publications, 1991.

Eric Siegel, Brian Ford and Jay Bornstein, *The Ernst & Young Business Plan Guide* (2nd. edition). New York: John Wiley & Sons, 1993.

Financial Scorekeeping

Career Press editors, *Understanding the Bottom Line* (2nd. edition). Hawthorne, New Jersey: Career Press, 1993.

David H. Bangs Jr., *Financial Troubleshooting: An Action Plan for Money Management in the Small Business.* Dover, New Hampshire: Upstart Press.

Phyllis Berman, Nancy Rotenier, "Sullivan's Ordeals." *Forbes*, September 27, 1993.

Gary Brenner et al., *The Complete Handbook for the Entrepreneur.* New Jersey: Prentice Hall Publishing, 1990.

Jefferey Davidson, Charles Dean, *Cash Traps: Small Business Secrets for Reducing Costs & Improving Cash Flow.* New York: John Wiley & Sons, 1991.

James Henderson, *Obtaining Venture Financing and Practices.* New York: The Free Press, 1992.

Robert Hisrich, Candida Brush, *The Woman Entrepreneur: Starting, Financing, and Managing a Successful New Business.* Massachusetts: Lexington Books, 1986.

Joseph Mancuso, *How to Write a Winning Business Plan.* New Jersey: Prentice-Hall, 1990.

Stanley Rich, David Gumpert, *Business Plans That Win $$$: Lessons from the MIT Enterprise Forum*. New York: Harper-Collins, 1989.

John Tracy, *How to Read a Financial Report: Wringing Vital Signs Out of the Numbers*. New York: John Wiley & Sons, 1993.

Dana Wechsler Linden, Nancy Rotenier, "Good-bye to Berle & Means." *Forbes*, January 3, 1994.

Marketing and Sales

Scott A. Clark, *Beating the Odds: Ten Smart Steps to Small Business Success*. AMACOM, 1991.

Brett Kingstone, *Student Entrepreneur's Guide: How to Start & Run Your Own Business*. McGraw-Hill, 1990.

Jay Levinson, Seth Godin, *The Guerilla Marketing Handbook*. New York: Houghton Mifflin, 1994.

Jay Levinson, *Guerilla Marketing for the Nineties: The Newest Secrets for Making Big Profits from Your Small Business*. New York: Houghton Mifflin, 1993.

Jay Levinson, *Guerilla Marketing Attack*. New York: Houghton Mifflin, 1989.

Lyle Maul and Dianne Mayfield, *The Entrepreneur's Road Map*. New York: Saxtons River Publications, 1990.

Don Peppers, *One to One Future: Building Relationships One Customer at a Time*. New York: Doubleday, 1993.

Michael Porter, *Competitive Advantage*. New York, MacMillan.

Product Development

Thomas Davenport, *Process Innovation: Re-engineering Work through Information Technology*. Massachusetts: Harvard University Press, 1993.

Stephen C. Harper, *The McGraw-Hill Guide to Starting Your Own Business: A Step-by-Step Blueprint for the First-Time Entrepreneur*. McGraw-Hill, 1991.

Marco Iansiti, "Real-World R&D: Jumping the Product Generation Gap." *Harvard Business Review*, May-June 1993.

Donald Kuratko and Richard Hodgetts, *Entrepreneurship: A Contemporary Approach.* Fort Worth: Dryden Press.

Ronald Merrill, Henry Sedgwick, *The New Venture Handbook: Everything You Need to Know To Start and Run Your Own Business.* New York: AMACOM, 1987.

Robert Tomasko, *Rethinking the Corporation: The Architecture of Change.* New York: AMACOM, 1993.

Mel Ziegler, Bill Rosenzweig, Patricia Ziegler, *The Republic of Tea: Letters to a Young Zentrepreneur.* New York: Currency/Doubleday, 1992.

Operations

Ken Blanchard, Sheldon Bowles, *Raving Fans.* New York: William Morrow & Co., 1993.

Bill Creech, *The Five Pillars of TQM: How to Make Total Quality Management Work for You.* New York: NAL-Dutton, 1994.

William H. Davidow and Michael Malone, *The Virtual Corporation.* New York: HarperCollins, 1992.

Robert Frey, "Empowerment or Else." *Harvard Business Review*, September-October 1993.

Eliyahu Goldratt, Jeff Cox, *The Goal.* Croton-on-Hudson, New York: North River Press, Inc., 1986.

Michael Hammer and James Champy, *Reengineering the Corporation: A Manifesto for Business Revolution.* New York: Harper Business, 1994.

Richard M. Hodgetts, *Blueprints for Continuous Improvement: Lessons from the Baldrige Winners.* New York: American Management Association, 1993.

Joseph Juran, *Juran's New Quality Road Map: Planning, Setting, & Reaching Quality Goals.* New York: The Free Press, 1992.

Joseph Juran, Frank Gryna (editors), *Juran's Quality Control Handbook* (4th edition). New York: McGraw-Hill Books, 1988.

Joseph Juran, *Juran on Leadership for Quality: An Executive Handbook*. New York: The Free Press, 1989.

Fred Luthans, "Meeting the New Paradigm Challenges through Total Quality Management." *Management Quarterly*, Spring 1993.

Jeremy Main (editor), *The Road to Quality: A Juran Institute Report*. New York: The Free Press, 1994.

Richard J. Schonberger, *World Class Manufacturing*. New York: The Free Press, 1986.

Peter Senge, *Fifth Discipline*. New York: Currency/Doubleday, 1990.

Robert Sibson, *Maximizing Employee Productivity: A Managers Guide*. New York: AMACOM, 1994.

COMPUTER SOFTWARE

Setting Direction

Developing a Successful Business Plan. Entrepreneur Magazine, Virgin Mastertronics (800-874-4607).

VenturPlan: Retail and *VenturPlan: Service*. Boston: Venture Software. (617) 491-6156

Setting Budgets

How to Write a Business Plan. Minneapolis: The American Institute of Small Business. (800-328-2906)

Ronstadt's Financials. Dover, Massachusetts: Lord Publishing Co.

Taxcalc Business Planning Model for Forecast and Projections. 800-527-2669.

Financial Scorekeeping

Art of Negotiation. Berkeley, California: Experience in Software Inc.

Daniel Bernstein, *Negotiator Pro.*

Tim Berry, *Business Plan Toolkit.* Palo Alto, California: Palo Alto Software. (800-229-7526)

PlanMaker. St. Louis, Missouri: PowerSolutions for Business.

Value Express. San Diego, California: ValueSource, Inc.

Marketing

Business Insight. Austin, Texas: Business Resource Software Inc.

INDEX

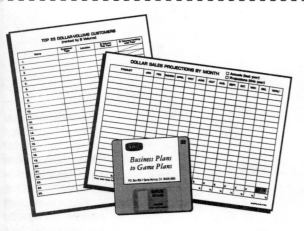

BUSINESS REPLY CARD

FIRST CLASS MAIL PERMIT NO. 243 SANTA MONICA, CA

POSTAGE WILL BE PAID BY ADDRESSEE

 **THE MERRITT COMPANY**
POST OFFICE BOX 955
SANTA MONICA, CA 90406-9875

SWAD

BUSINESS REPLY CARD

FIRST CLASS MAIL PERMIT NO. 243 SANTA MONICA, CA

POSTAGE WILL BE PAID BY ADDRESSEE

 **THE MERRITT COMPANY**
POST OFFICE BOX 955
SANTA MONICA, CA 90406-9875

SWAE